A Mystical Trilogy ~ 2

Why are we alive?

Our Search for Meaning

~ Book 2 ~

'Awaken to the meaning of life through this
three-book series of clear, heartfelt
spiritual reflections on spirituality,
enlightenment, and the journey within'.

By Ken Luball

Author's Note

"Why are we alive?" This timeless question lies at the heart of *'Our Search for Meaning' – Book 2.* Written in clear, easily understandable language, these 250 free verse poems use metaphor, imagery, and spiritual insight to explore themes of awakening, enlightenment, and the human pursuit of meaning, as it guides readers toward a deeper understanding of life's true purpose.

My hope writing: *'Our Search for Meaning'* was to try to awaken and help others who are awakened more fully understand what enlightenment is so their journey through life may be more fully realized.

As you prepare to begin your search for meaning, do so with an open heart and mind, ready to delve deeper into the mysteries of existence. Let us embark on this **spiritual** adventure together, and, in doing so, discover the answers you are searching for.

Glossary

Asleep – After we are born we are taught how to survive in the world and what success is. We therefore learn to worry only about our own success and survival in the world, rather than to be concerned about others. This results in living in a self-centered world of prejudice, inequity, and endless struggle. Those who fully believe this are asleep, accepting the status quo as the truth.

Awaken – There may come a time in our life when, despite our success in the world, we begin to question the truth of our self-centered learned beliefs, our ego. When this happens the first quiet messages of the spirit, a piece of god present within every life are sensed, beginning us on an enduring journey to discover meaning in our life.

Ego – The ego is everything we learn, believe, and accept is true after we are born, as we learn how to survive in a self-centered world. Its primary concern is what is best for us; it worries little about others. It also attempts to build up our self-esteem by convincing us of our value in the world.

Enlightenment – The complete acceptance of the spiritual path, allowing the spirit's inherent wisdom and unconditional love to be our primary guide in life. With enlightenment, the ego, our self-centered learned beliefs, assumes a secondary role in our life, no longer influencing the direction of our life choices.

Spirit/ Soul/ God / Higher-Self – An ethereal entity accompanying and inextricably connecting every life to another's. Its purpose is to give our lives meaning by sharing its inherent wisdom and unconditional love to help guide our life's choices.

Spirituality – Spirituality is the belief there is a piece of god, a spirit or soul within every life intimately linking each of us to the other, and, because of this, each life, regardless of our differences, accomplishments, or genus, is important, equal, and connected.

The Mountain Top

Surrounded by towering white
covered peaks, the snow
begins to melt in spring.
Its water flows, rippling past rocks
downhill in streams, sustaining
the many forest inhabitants.
To reach the mountain summit,
an arduous climb is required; sheer
rock cliffs, high winds, freezing
temperatures, present themselves
as the mountain top is near.

We begin our lives on top of
the mountain with spectacular
views of the world below.
As we are taught about life
though, and what is expected of
us, our view begins to diminish;
we begin to descend the mountain
as we accept the truth of
what we learned growing up.
By the time we reach the base of
The mountain, accepting all of
society's self-centered viewpoints,
we have forgotten what the beautiful
scenic view on the peak looked like.

We may only begin to reclimb the
mountain when we begin to question

if what we had learned and accepted
during our lives was true.
Once we realize and acknowledge
little of it was, we may once again
be able to reach the summit, and
appreciate the beautiful views
of the world below, as we
were always meant to do.

The Sword and the Shield

We are born free, though as
we are exposed to the world
and its beliefs, we each acquire
a sword and a shield to protect
us from life's injustices.
Our shield deflects injurious
rage, preventing others words
and deeds from hurting us.
Our sword is our response,
as its sharp blade attempts to
penetrate another's defenses.
These self-centered tools
prevent us from ever
discovering genuine love
and meaning in our lives.

Only by yielding, putting down
our instruments of conflict,
will our true purpose in
life become evident.
With this surrender, though our
learned beliefs will remain, they
will no longer direct our actions.
Rather, our spirit present within
each life, free from its confines
behind our sword and shield,
will now be permitted to
reveal our true destiny.

Our Sixth Sense

Most people imagine and
live their entire lives believing
there are only five senses: hearing,
touch, sight, taste, and smell.
Those who do, though they may
have led a good life and been
successful, have neglected the
most important sense, our
sixth sense: the spirit.
Also known as soul, god, our
higher-self, it opens life to a
whole new dimension of thought,
beliefs, and understanding.

Our sixth sense permits us to
find genuine meaning in our
lives by allowing us to
discover and selflessly
share our loving core present
within every life.
Doing so is the reason we
are born, the true meaning
of our life's journey.

The Comfort of Silence

When we see a wrong, do or
say nothing, we are contributing
to the decline of our world.
Many have different opinions
as to what is considered wrong.
Spiritually, morally, and ethically,
wrong is doing anything to
harm another in any way.
It matters not if the injury is
physical, verbal, or ignoring
the many human offenses
we inflict on each other.
War, hunger, homelessness;
prejudice, inequity, hate.

These and many more human
transgressions are caused by
our comfort of silence, fearful
of saying something to
upset the status quo.

We must be silent no more.
Every indiscretion must be
met and challenged with
resistance, speaking up loudly
in defense of those being harmed.
If we see anything we would not
wish to happen to us or those
we are closest to, that is the
measure to be silent no more.

Our Second Act

There may come a time in
our lives when we begin to
reevaluate everything we
once believed important.
Despite living a successful
life, having family, prestige,
money, material possessions,
a sense begins to emerge making
us question if there is more
to life than what we were
taught and achieved.
We awaken.

Often, this moment presents
an opportunity for our second
act in life to begin, as we
reevaluate our job, relationships,
beliefs, and everything else we
once believed to be true.
This feeling comes from our
spirit within and may cause
our lives to unravel as we
begin to question all
our choices in life.

Once we awaken, we may
never fall back asleep.
We begin to view the world
differently; one where we
realize our definition of

success was distorted.
Money, prestige, family, no
longer dominate our self-
centered view of the world.
Our second act in life begins
when we understand selflessly
helping others also find
success in the world is
the genuine reason
for our life's journey.

The Baker

I woke up at 3 a.m. every
day for the past 45 years to
prepare and bake cakes, bread,
and other delicious pastries
to sell in my bakery.
I am now in the twilight of life.
Where have all the years gone?
As I sit on my porch, I
begin to understand I spent
those years working, buying
things to make my life
easier, paying bills.
Is this all there is to life?

If you answer yes, then,
like me, our lives have
not been fully lived.
We simply went through
the motions, doing everything
we were taught to live
a successful life.
It is only now, as death nears,
I finally understand there is
so much more I was
supposed to accomplish.
I never genuinely knew love,
inner peace, or happiness.
Though I thought I did,
had a family, traveled,

did fun things, these
emotions eluded me as
I only experienced
them superficially.

Though it is too late for
me, I now realize these
genuine emotions
have always been
part of me.
All I had to do to
experience them was
open my heart, then
selflessly share them
with others.

Perhaps if I had done
this, spent less time
burying my head in the
oven the pastries were
baked in, I would have
realized sooner, there
was so much more to life
than just doing what
I had been told.

The Storm

The darkening clouds
above threaten the
peaceful earth below.
As the first drops of rain
begin to fall, many race
for shelter to avoid being
caught in its wake.
As the deluge increases,
the howling wind intensifies
the storms ferocity.
Many barely notice the
weather, safe, comfortable
in their abode.

There are others though,
the discarded, the untouchables,
ignored by society due to
poverty or their life
situation, who become
drenched from the
unrelenting wind and
rain, having no shelter
to protect them from
the elements.

An enlightened society
would not allow anyone
to stand alone in the storm.
Rather, they would

provide refuge to protect
everyone, regardless of
our differences or their
circumstances in life.

To truly change the world,
we must selflessly embrace
the outcasts, the discarded,
allowing them to find protection
from the storm as well.

A Long and Winding Road

There are many turns,
curves, and detours we
encounter on our
journey through life.
The final destination though,
is the same: the reunification
with our spirit, present
within every life.

How we get there is
influenced by our
experiences and acceptance
of what we were taught and
consider to be the truth.
The more we believe our
self-centered views are
genuine, the sharper the
turns in the road will be,
making our journey
longer, more challenging.

For those who start to
question these truths,
beginning to sense a
presence within, the turns
and detours in the road lessen;
its end may now become visible.
Though few will reach the end of
the road, it is the journey getting
there that is life's true purpose.

What is the Purpose of the Spirit?

The spirit is an ethereal
entity accompanying every
life, present to share its
inherent wisdom and
unconditional love to
allow our lives to have
genuine meaning and purpose.
The spirit may be considered
to be our higher-self,
a piece of god.
It often is in competition
with the self, our learned beliefs.

Without the spirit, without
striving to become one with
our higher-self, all that is
left are our experiences
 and survival techniques
learned since we were born.
Meaning found in a self-
centered world is an illusion.
It may only be discovered by
accepting and selflessly
sharing the wisdom and
pure loving messages
of the spirit within.

The Door

Imagine a hill with a
door on the top.
On one side of the hill,
at its base, are our self-
centered beliefs.
When we are here, the
hill is very steep and
difficult to climb.

As our spirit, the source
of divine wisdom and
intuition within us, becomes
a little stronger, and we
begin to awaken, the incline
of the hill appears less severe;
we may begin to ascend it
in an effort to approach
the door on the top.

We know if we can reach
the door and go through it,
we will find enlightenment
on the other side, becoming
one with our higher-self.
Though, at times, we may
briefly pass through the door,
the stress and anxieties
of life soon return, and
we find ourselves being

dragged back through the
door once more, falling
back down the hill.

Only by fully embracing
the wisdom and unconditional
loving messages of our spirit
within, then selflessly sharing
them with others, may we
remain on the other side
of the door, and in doing
so, realize our true
purpose in life.

Chi (Qi)

Every life has two forms.
The physical form
is the body, mortal,
beginning at conception,
ending with death.
There is also essence
present within every life.
The essence is immortal,
joining each life in the
beginning and returning
to a higher vibrational
level when the body dies.

Though these appear to
be separate, chi is the
bridge connecting
them together.
Both will exist,
influencing us
throughout our brief life.
When our physical form,
with its emotions, thoughts,
and beliefs dominate, our
chi is weakened, often
resulting in stress,
hardship, and anxiety.
When our essence, however,
dominates, our future brightens.

To embrace the power,
the energy of our chi,
accept the spiritual path
through life, unleashing
the force of our spirit's
inherent wisdom and
unconditional love,
allowing us to begin
a journey to discover
our life's genuine purpose.

The Messages Within

We need not travel,
amass material possessions,
have a lot of money, or
anything else that may
be found in the world
to find genuine
happiness, meaning,
love, and inner peace.
Though many endlessly
search for these in a self-
centered world, they
may not be found there.

To discover where they
truly exist, sit in a
comfortable chair,
silence your mind,
listen to the quiet
messages in between
your racing thoughts,
then selflessly share
the wisdom and
unconditional love you
sense with the world.

Religious Divisions

Easter, Passover, Ramadan.
Christian, Jewish, Muslim.
These are but three of many
religions dividing, rather
than uniting the world.
The differences have led
to prejudice, wars,
indifference to the
struggles of those
who believe differently.

Though each may have
differing views on god,
the underlying message
they voice has been lost.
It is a message of unselfishly
helping and loving others,
guaranteeing the right of
everyone to be safe, have
food to eat, a home to live
in, a planet that will not be
destroyed by greed and apathy.
It is treating every person,
regardless of our beliefs,
and all forms of life, with
the same respect we wish
for ourselves.

Perhaps it is time to put

our self-centered learned
religious beliefs aside,
embracing instead the
initial spiritual messages
Jesus, Moses, and Mohammed,
had originally intended
for us to adopt.
A message of unconditional
love, selflessly shared with
others, for the benefit of all.

The Barrier to Enlightenment

When we are awakened,
we realize more than
just the self is present
and influencing us.
We begin to understand
the spirit exists as well.

What prevents an
awakened person from
reaching enlightenment
is this knowledge is
not fully accepted.
There is still a belief,
fostered by the self,
that meaning, happiness,
and inner peace may be
found in a self-centered
world; it cannot.

It must first be
discovered within,
then it must be shared
without motive or
benefit, with all others.

Our Higher-Self

The reason we are
born, what our higher-
self represents, is a
return to the inherent
knowledge and
unconditional love
present within every
life before our birth,
unimpeded by the
distraction's life presents us.

Our spirit teaches us to
be selfless, loving,
compassionate to
everyone, regardless
of our differences.
It lets us know every
life is equally important,
and only by helping each
other unselfishly will
the struggles we may
have after we are born
lessen, and the genuine
meaning of our life's
journey be understood.

Every Life is Meaningful

With enlightenment,
the disguises others
wear fade away.
The negativity of life
wanes, seeing the best
in others, rather than
only their flaws.
The desire to improve
the world by helping
others is overwhelming.

With this understanding
we realize every life is
intimately connected by
a spirit, a piece of god
within, and each life
therefore, regardless
of our differences, has
purpose and meaning.

The Irony of Life

When we are first
born, we know only
unconditional love.
None of the harsh
realities of the self-
centered world have
yet distorted our pure
hopeful vision of life.
With our socialization
into the world though,
we will never return to
the innocence we once
knew before our birth.

The irony of life is we
may then spend the rest
of our lives undoing the
damage done during our
earliest years when our
views, beliefs, prejudices,
and opinions of the
world are formed,
trying desperately
to return to the
loving, peaceful
moment we once
knew before we
were first born.

The Divide

Our world is endlessly
divided into castes.
Religion, ethnicity,
race, wealth, are just
a few of the many
divisions in a self-
centered world too
obsessed to notice
or care.
These division are used
to justify the superiority
of some over others.
They are also the primary
cause of war, prejudice,
inequity, and many of
humanity's other problems.

In spirituality there
are no castes.
Every life, though
different in appearance,
beliefs, genus, is equally
valuable, deserving to be
treated with respect and
unconditional love.
Only when this is
recognized and accepted,
may the spiritual evolution
of our planet finally begin.

The Reflection Pond

Look at yourself as
you gaze into a calm
pool of water; peer
deeply into your eyes.
Beyond the pretense,
the façade we present
to the world, a sentient
being may be seen.
Its purpose is to share
its inherent knowledge
and unconditional love
with us, allowing our
life to be led with true
purpose and meaning.

Only when we selflessly
share this part of
ourselves with others,
will the genuine reason
for our presence be
truly understood.

Our True Path

From the moment
we are born, with
our first breath,
everything changes.
At that very instant,
the ego, our self-centered
beliefs, is created.
Everything we see and
are exposed to throughout
our life will help
strengthen the ego.
Accepting what we are
taught will be the cause
of many challenges we
may face and in allowing
us to find true meaning
in our life.

We are born enlightened,
with the inherent knowledge
and unconditional love
of the spirit, a piece
of god within.
It is not until we are
socialized to accept the
mores of society, we
forget our true purpose.

Everything we have

learned from our birth
are obstacles, encouraged
by the ego, to detour us
from the genuine path
through life we are meant
to follow: the spiritual path.
With this understanding,
we awaken, beginning us
on an unending journey
toward enlightenment.

When the Wind Blows

The wind may be calm,
gently blowing the
leaves of trees, as they
majestically sway in
the soothing breeze.
It also may be fierce,
causing enormous
damage as storms emerge
across our planet.

Just as the wind gusts,
we often have moments
in life affecting how
intense our stress
and emotions are.
In times of balance,
we are steady.
There are periods in
our lives, however, our
reactions may be extreme.
When these occur, no
longer in control, we
may act out, harming
others with our words,
actions, or deeds.

To calm the winds, we
must begin to understand
there is another force

active in our life
besides the wind; it
is the spirit, a piece
of god present
within every life.
With this realization,
we awaken.

With the acceptance
and guidance of our
spirit's inherent wisdom
and unconditional loving
beliefs, the wind calms,
enabling us to journey
further in our quest to
discover our genuine
purpose in life.

I Am Human

There are those who
believe the lives of
human beings are more
important than other
forms of life, and that
some people, due to
their differences, are
better than others.
Some embrace our
differences to justify
their beliefs and actions.

In reality, though we
may believe, look, act
differently, or we may
be a different genus,
we each possess a piece
of the divine within,
inextricably connecting
each of us to the other.
We have never been
greater or our lives
more significant than
anyone else or any other
life form; each possesses
a spirit, a piece of
god within as well.

Understanding this,

sharing our spirit's
inherent wisdom and
unconditional love to
selflessly help others
in need, is the lesson
we are alive to learn.

The Answers

The ego, our self-
centered beliefs,
tells us everything
we need can be
found in the world.
If we even partially
believe this, though
we may have awoken,
sensing the first
messages from our
spirit, enlightenment
will remain elusive.

The spirit, however,
asks us to seek our
answers within, where
they have always been,
and then to selflessly
share the wisdom and
unconditional love present
there with all others.

It is ironic, most spend
their entire life searching
for meaning in the
world; it may not
be found there.
We have always
had the answers.

We were simply looking for
them in the wrong place.
We only had to open our
hearts, listen to the quiet
loving messages of our
spirit within, and we would
have understood this.

Here Comes the Sun

Over the nearby snow-
covered mountain peaks,
the first rays of the sun
bring light and warmth
to an indifferent self-
centered world.
It shines its light on all
living things in its
proximity, bringing hope
to those who value its purpose.
It does not discriminate
on who receives its gifts,
presenting its light to help
plants and animals thrive
and warmth to benefit
all living things on
our fragile world.

We are the sun.
With our warmth and
light, we may each
change the world by
selflessly sharing our
radiance and unconditional
love to improve the
lives of all.

Listen to the Silence

We all wish to be heard;
it is part of being human.
Yet it is not what we
say that is important.
Rather, it is what we hear
when we genuinely listen
to the messages behind
the words being said.

If we listen intently, we
may hear the underlying
meaning, hidden deep
within the realm of
the subconscious,
not disguised by our
self-centered opinions.
If we remain quiet, we
may hear the authentic
messages of the spirit,
accompanying each on
their life's journey.
It is a message of
unconditional love,
hope, and sincere desire
for us to hear the
messages from our
own spirit as well.

Life Lessons

During our lives we
learn many lessons
about life that influence
our decisions and the
path we will take as we
strive to be happy,
successful, and live
a meaningful life.

If our experiences and
choices reinforce our
self-centered desire to
do only what is best for
ourself, then our goals in
life will never be realized.

Happiness, success, and
meaning may not be found
in a self-centered world.
They must first be
discovered within,
then selflessly shared,
without reservation,
with all others.

Only then will we not
only find what we desire,
but also discover the lesson
we are here to learn, the true
purpose of our life's journey.

Which Path Will We Follow?

There are but two
paths through life
we each may pursue.
We may either follow
the self-centered path
of the ego, our learned
beliefs; or we may seek
the spiritual path, the
one we were always
meant to follow.

The former idolizes money.
Its primary concern is for
our individual success in
life, often defined by
material possessions
and other things we
were told would make
our lives worthwhile.

Those pursuing a
spiritual path, however,
though they may have
little money or possessions,
are equally concerned about
every life and how they
may sincerely help others.

We each choose which

path through life to
follow; we may change
our path at any time.
One path may lead to
success in the world,
though to leading a
life lacking meaning.
The other, though not
outwardly successful,
will lead to true inner
peace, happiness, love,
and discovering the
genuine purpose for
our life's journey.

Fear

Though fear may be
inherent, such as our
fight or flight reaction
to danger, there is also
acquired fear we learn
and worry about as
we are brought up
to be afraid of others.

This fear often is the
underlying cause of hate,
prejudice, war, and most
other negative emotions.
It results in a world of
needless death, hunger,
inequity, and numerous
unnecessary struggles by
many throughout history.

Only by selflessly
embracing love rather
than fear, accepting the
inherent good within
every life, will we be
able to break this
relentless cycle,
allowing our children
to live in a world of
peace rather than conflict.

Hiding From Pain

Many choose to hide
from the hardships of
life we each must confront.
They may wear a mask,
metaphorically covering
their face to hide their
true feelings and
emotions from others.

They may also conceal
themselves behind a wall
they erected within to
protect them from the
pain of living in a harsh
often cruel world, where
words, deeds, and
actions, may cause
stress, anxiety, and despair.

In addition to the mask
and wall, some may take
drugs, drink alcohol, or
find other ways to hide
their authentic-self,
from the world.
Living like this isolates
us not only from our
acquaintances, but from
friends, close family,

and even ourselves.
Though we may be
surrounded by many
others, we are truly
alone, hiding from the
world, isolating who we
really are from all others.

We are each spirit.
The rest is simply an
illusion created by the
ego, our learned beliefs,
to help disguise our
genuine purpose in life.

It is only when we decide
to stop hiding, may we
finally find what we have
sought our entire lives:
happiness, unconditional
love, inner peace, and a
genuine understanding
of our life's true purpose.

The Rain

The rain is gently
falling on an overcast
cloudy day.
Each drop splashes
as it reaches the ground,
helping nourish the
earth and provide water
to all who live on it.
Though a single raindrop
helps to slightly replenish
the rivers and quench the
thirst of one, alone it cannot
sustain life by itself.
Only combined with other
raindrops, will it be able to
satisfy the needs of many.

We each are like a
single raindrop.
Alone, we are isolated,
struggling to survive in
a self-centered world.
Together, however,
selflessly helping each
other, the needs of all
may be met, allowing
each to not only endure,
but thrive as well.

Wealth

Many believe wealth is
having a lot of money,
material possessions,
being able to do the
best things life offers.
Though having these
make life easier, in truth,
wealth has little to do
with any of them.
This belief is an illusion
we accepted as real when
we were taught what
success and wealth are
in a self-centered world.

Real wealth comes from
within, and is only acquired
when we selflessly share
the wisdom and
unconditional
love of our spirit
with all others.

With this understanding
of what true wealth is,
our riches will be unearthed,
as we experience genuine
love, inner peace, and
discover the true
meaning of life.

Living in a Bubble

While we mature
within our mother,
we are enclosed in
an amniotic sac to
protect and provide
nourishment to us
until we are ready to
enter the world.
With our birth, no longer
requiring its help,
it is discarded.

It does not take long,
though, for another sac
to form, a bubble around
us, protecting us from
emotional pain and
nourishing our self-esteem.
This bubble is the ego,
our learned beliefs, and
it is reinforced by our
socialization into a self-
centered world.
Though this bubble
defends and nurtures us,
it also isolates us from
each other and from
our authentic-self.

As long as the bubble is
intact, even if its walls
are thin, we will continue
to struggle to find
meaning in our lives.
It is only when we burst
the bubble, as we once
did upon our birth, we
may begin a quest to
discover our true
purpose in life.

Building a Wall or a Bridge

In life, we may choose
whether to build a
wall or a bridge.
The wall isolates us
from not only each
other, but from
ourself as well.
It hides the beauty in
the distance of faraway
mountain tops, meandering
rivers, and open meadows
full of flowers.
Instead we find a barrier
we cannot see through,
blocking our view of
the world's grandeur.

The bridge is quite different.
Rather than dividing us,
it connects all life
to each other.
In the distance, the views
remain unobstructed as
we are able to see through
it to the other side.

If we view the world
through a wall, having
only a partial view of it

as we peer over the
top, we will only see
a superficial image, a
façade, we each
project to others.
When we see a world
full of bridges though,
instead of walls, we see
kindness, unconditional
love, present within
every life, desiring only
to selflessly help all others.

To change the future and
further the spiritual
evolution of our planet,
we must tear down all
our isolating walls,
replacing them instead
with bridges that will
connect us all together.

The Will of God

God is known by
many names.
Spirit, soul, higher-self,
are but three spiritual names
synonymous with god.
Allah, Jehovah, Yahweh,
are also known as god in
three prominent world religions.

Though many know god
by different names, god
has only one underlying
message uniting each:
sharing unconditional
love with all.
The will of god does not
tolerate hate, intolerance,
self-centered greed.
Nor does it condone
allowing needless
death due to starvation,
war, indifference.
Or the struggles of so
many due to poverty,
homelessness, prejudice.

God is love.
Believing in god means
equally sharing and

selflessly helping
everyone, regardless
of our differences, and
treating all other forms
of life and mother earth
with the respect she deserves.

This is the will of god.
Anything else is a learned
illusion, propagated by
organized religion, that
long ago lost sight of
the true meaning and
beliefs god intended.

A Candle in the Wind

A calm breeze gently
blows the flame of a
candle flickering its
light and warmth on
all surrounding it.
The candle connects
each together with
its mystifying glow.

We are all candles in
the wind, intimately
connected by a universal
spirit, uniting us as one
in our brief journey
through life.

Only by selflessly
helping each other
will our light become
brighter and our life
more meaningful.

The Eyes of a Spirit

A spirit, a piece
of god dwells
within every life.
It views the world
with unconditional
love, meant to be
selflessly shared
with all others.
There are no
alternative motives
or emotions.
The eyes of a spirit
see beyond the façade
others project, directly
hearing the messages of
the other's spirit within.

When we are attentive
to our spirit, we sense
the true meaning of
another, as it effortlessly
communicates silently with
the other's divine presence.
To really know another,
be silent, listen quietly
to the genuine meaning
you sense in between
your racing thoughts.
It is only then you will
know what they are truly saying.

Some Days We Eat

I am four years old today.
Though it is my birthday,
my family cannot afford
to buy me a cake or presents.
We are quite poor, do not
have a home to live in
or warm clothes to wear.
Many days we do not
have any food to eat
either, though my parents
try to earn money.
We are homeless; I
am always afraid.
Some days, I walk past
others like us, who died
during the night from
sickness, lack of food,
or being hurt by someone else.

I wonder why our family
and others have to
live like this.
I dream to be like other
children who have a home,
food to eat every day,
clothes to wear that
keep them warm.
I do not understand why
they do not help us and

others like us who
are not as fortunate.
Are these people
better than us?
Are their lives more
important because they
have more money?
I do not believe they are.

If I were in charge of
the world, everyone
would share what they
have so no one would
need to struggle as we are.
This is the world we
live in, though it does
not need to be.
We are meant selflessly
share our wealth and
excess, allowing everyone,
regardless of our differences
or accomplishments, to be
helped in their time of need,
so no one needlessly suffers.
This is the spiritual path
through life we were
always meant to follow.
This is the lesson we
are here to learn.

Darkness and Light

Darkness is not within.
It comes from the self-
centered world around
us and is internalized.
Within there is only light.
Darkness, learned after
we are born, dominates
the views and actions of
most, causing many of
the man-made problems
in the world.

Though darkness will
always remain throughout
our life, it need not
control our choices.
It is only when we
allow light to direct
our actions, becoming
our primary guide in life,
the world may finally
evolve, allowing our
children to grow up in
a world of peace rather
than war, tolerance
rather than prejudice,
and love rather than hate.

We Are God

If there is a definition
of god, it would be
the totality of all
spirits connected to
each other by their
proximity and,
therefore, existing
as one entity.
This one entity,
present in an alternate
plane of existence at a
higher vibrational level,
may be considered to be god.

To take this discussion one
step further, every spirit
would therefore represent
a piece or part of god.
Since there is a spirit
within everyone and
everything alive, there
is a part or piece of
god within every
life as well.

Look Beyond the Façade

When you see someone,
look beyond the façade.
See the good within; the
pretense is not real.
It is a fiction created
by the ego, our learned
beliefs, from everything
we have learned and
accepted as true
in our life.

Despite our
accomplishments
or differences,
every life is equally
valuable, intimately
connected by a
universal spirit within.
To truly know another,
see the genuine soul within.

When Children Start Dying

How can the
senseless death of
even one child be
acceptable?
Whether that child
died in war, from
starvation, a treatable
illness, or in any other
manner, their loss will
be suffered by everyone;
their essence within no
longer present to shine
their light on the world.
This is true not only of
children, but every
life as well.

Is someone's life,
because of their wealth,
fame, job, ethnicity, race,
or any other comparison,
more valuable than
another's who is poor,
homeless, a minority?
If you answered yes,
then you have found a
way to rationalize
our children dying.

If you answered no
though, perhaps it is
time to awaken,
understanding every
life is, and always has
been, equally valuable
and those most
vulnerable, our children,
their light must never
again be allowed to
senselessly darken.

The Illusion

Life is an illusion,
beginning when
we are young, as
we are taught how to
survive in the world.
We learn from every
interaction we have
in our daily lives.
These ideas form the
basis of the person we
are to become, often for
the remainder our life.
The ego, our learned
beliefs, teaches us to
accept the self-centered
status quo of the world
in which we live.
Those doing so, remain
asleep, living in a
world of deception.

With enlightenment,
the illusions we were
taught and accepted
as real are exposed.
The egocentric world
of the matrix dissolves,
truth in its wake.
Little we learned

in life was true.

Truth may not be
discovered in a self-
centered world.
It only lies within, where
it has always been.
Then, it must be
selflessly shared with
others to help them
discover truth in
their life as well.

The Elder

With age, the
inevitability of
death creeps closer.
Now, considered elders
in society, many review
the life they had lived.
Material possessions,
prestige, beliefs, wealth,
begin to have less meaning.

Those who have lived a
successful life are not
immune to this review;
death does not favor them.
At this time, some may
finally begin to understand
their definition of success
may have been flawed.
Achieving success in the
world to only benefit
ourselves has not made
their lives meaningful
or important.
In fact, they may start
to realize the exact
opposite is true.

The elder may begin
to sense a message

within telling them
true success in life may
only be experienced by
selflessly helping others
become successful in
their life as well.

Thoughts and Prayers

After a preventable
tragedy, observing
children and others
dying from senseless
violence, how many
more times must we
hear "our thoughts and
prayers are with
those who died."
These heartbreaking
deaths are avoidable,
caused the greed and
desire for power of the
few and the acceptance
by the rest of the status quo.

Any law or action taken
should have only one
underlying consideration;
what is best for everyone,
not just the select few.
Every life is equally important.
It matters not our race,
wealth, beliefs or any
other comparison we
may make; each deserves
to be treated with respect
and unconditional love,
helped in their time of need.

Only when this is
finally realized and
accepted will thoughts
and prayers for avertable
tragedies no longer be
necessary, and the
spiritual evolution of
humanity become reality.

Emotions

After we are born
we learn what happiness,
love, and other emotions
are by observing
those around us.
Though we may
believe we understand
what they are, we do not.

Learned emotions are
conditional, often
reflected by our own
desires and needs.
Only unconditional
emotions, inherent
within each life,
selflessly shared
without pause or
benefit, are genuine.

To truly know
another, gaze deeply
within their soul,
where these dormant
emotions, long hidden
from view, have
always been.

Waking Up From A Dream

Many go through
life asleep, living in
a twilight fog cloaking
their vision of life.
Those living like this,
believe and accept
everything they learned
about life was true.

Despite their success
in the world though,
there may come a time
in their life they begin
to question if what
they learned was true.
A feeling deep within,
begins to emerge
wondering if there is
more to life than success.
At this point, they
begin to awaken from
their lifelong slumber,
arousing them from
their dream, beginning
them on an enduring
journey toward enlightenment.

Spiritual Karma

There are those who
appear to evade justice,
committing deeds
harming others to
benefit themselves.
Though this may allow
them to be successful,
wealthy, powerful, it
does not allow them
to escape judgement.

Those who hurt others
in anyway, though they
may appear not to suffer
any consequences, having
achieved success in the
world, will never find
true happiness, love,
or meaning in their life.

As they approach death,
reviewing their life,
they will experience
the pain they caused to
every person throughout
their life and will then
realize, their life,
though successful, was led
without meaning or purpose.

The Eyes of a Child

When a child is born
and see the world for
the first time, their
eyes are wide open.
They know only one
emotion: unconditional
love meant to be shared
with all others.

From that very moment
though, when the child's
view of the world is
crystal clear, their eyes
begin to close, as they
are taught what to
believe in the self-
centered world they
are to live in.
The more the child
accepts what they learn,
the further their eyes
will close to the true
possibilities life offers.
There are some who
are blind; others who
must wear aids to
help them see.

The only thing in life

that is authentic is
unconditional love;
everything else is
an illusion.
When we truly
understand this,
we will be able to
fully reopen our
eyes once more,
as they were when
we were first born.

Which Way is the Wind Blowing?

Throughout our lives,
the wind gusts may
determine how
challenging our
life will be.
We discover our lives
are easiest when the
wind is blowing behind
us, allowing us to
effortlessly move forward.
When this happens, we
settle into a pattern
repeating our daily
routine, trying to enjoy
the benefits life brings.
We are content accepting
the status quo, believing
all we were taught is true.

As we approach death,
though we may have
had a good job, made
a lot of money, had a
family, and many material
possessions, when we
review our lives, we
may wonder where
the years have gone,
if our life truly

had meaning.
It is then we may
finally understand,
it did not.

Though it is much
more difficult, it is
only when we decide
to walk against the
wind, being equally
concerned for every
life, rather than only
our own, will we
discover the genuine
reason for our
life's journey.

Don't Follow the Crowd

From our first breath
we are taught to conform
to the beliefs of others.
We are told to only worry
and be concerned for
ourself as we learn
how to survive in a
self-centered world.
Though there are
some who are taught
about god through
their religious practices,
what they learned from
organized religion was
corrupted by man's
interpretation long ago.

Those who are
indoctrinated into
the world like this,
follow the crowd,
doing what is expected
of them to live a
successful life.
By following the
status quo, though
they may appear to
have led a good life,
they will have ignored

the lessons they
were born to learn.

Only when we no
longer follow the
crowd, realizing
little we were taught
was true, designed
to have us follow
a false path through
life, may we begin a
quest to discover the
genuine reason for
our life's journey.

Detours in Life

Life is like a winding
road on a steep slippery
mountain descent.
When we go too fast
or our tires simply cannot
grasp the road, our car
slides, as we desperately
try to stop it before it
goes over the side of
a mountain cliff.

Our lives are very
much the same.
Though we may
have planned our life,
diversions happen
causing our lives to
derail, changing the
course and direction
our life will take.
The death of a loved
one, loss of a job, or
unforeseen tragedy
may cause us to take
a detour in our life.

This time of struggle
offers a unique
opportunity to

reassess our lives.
If we embrace the
change, learn from
the new challenges,
we may discover our
lives were stagnant;
we had settled into
a repetitive routine.

With change, some
may begin to sense a
voice within, suggesting
a new path through life.
The messages they hear
talk of a path of service,
helping others, selflessly
sharing our excess and
love to help all who
are struggling through life.

Though loss is difficult,
embrace the opportunity
it provides to change
the direction of your
life and, by doing so,
discover enduring
inner peace,
unconditional love,
and the genuine
meaning of life.

The Caste System

Though humanity does not
acknowledge it, there is a
caste system dividing the
world, reflecting each
person's importance in it.
Those with a prestigious
job, wealth, fame; a certain
skin color, religion, ethnicity,
are considered the upper
caste simply because of
their success, beliefs,
or appearance.
Those who are poor,
live in impoverished
countries, do menial jobs, are
thought to be in the lowest class.

Most in the world fit in
between these two extremes.
The caste system is used to
justify how we treat others
and reward those who
have led a prosperous life.
This system though is the
underlying cause of most
man-made problems.
War, inequity, prejudice,
result from the need of
the few to justify their

superiority to others.

Only by ending this
egoistic practice,
understanding the
equal importance of
every life, regardless
of any differences,
may humanity awaken,
allowing the spiritual
evolution of our planet
to finally begin.

Choices in Life

There may come a
time in our life we
approach a fork
in the road.
If we take the straighter
less challenging road,
we may become
successful, have money,
material possessions,
a family, and other
symbols a thriving
life enjoys, as we
approach death, we
may find our life has
been lived without
purpose or meaning.

If, however, we take
the sharper curve at the
fork in the road, pursuing
a more difficult path
through life, though the
turn is much more
challenging, its path
quite curvaceous and
demanding, it will lead
to a genuine understanding
about our life's purpose.

The Iceberg

Every year, more
species become extinct.
Wars and senseless violence
continue, killing innocents.
Starving children, ribs
protruding from their
emaciated bodies,
needlessly die from
lack of nutrition.
Homeless, exposed to
danger and the elements,
vie for safety and shelter.
People dying from
treatable illness, too poor
to afford the cure.
The destruction of our
environment, leaving
an uninhabitable world
for our children to inherit.
Judgment of others due to
their race, religion, ethnicity.
Not sharing our surplus
with those in need; rather
hoarding it for ourselves
to enrich our own lives.

This list is but the tip of
the iceberg, barely visible
on top of the ocean, whose

mass lies miles below.
These things and much
more are caused by
humanity's self-centered
view of the world, ignoring
the iceberg, as long as
it does not affect them.

It is time we begin to
shrink the iceberg,
starting by selflessly
sharing our excess and
unconditional love to
help all in need.
Only then may these
problems begin to
mitigate and may our
world and all who
inhabit it begin to heal.

The Glass Ceiling

Above us, a clear glass
ceiling limits the distance
we may travel in our life.
Most of us live our entire
lives below this boundary,
inhibiting our ability to
experience what lies
beyond, above its confines.
Those who remain beneath
it, though they may view
what is above the ceiling,
accept everything they
learned about life, believing
success, meaning, and
happiness may be found in
the self-centered world;
it may not.

It is only when we break
the glass, soar above its
confines, we may finally
begin to recognize there is
more to understand about
life then what we were told.

Those who continue soaring
upward in the sky, reaching
the proximity of the universe,
realize everything we were

taught, all the learned truths
we accepted as true were
fictitious; understanding
genuine truth may only
be found within, then
must be selflessly shared,
without motive or
benefit, to help others
find truth in their
lives as well.

I Am Six Years Old

I am but one of billions
on a small planet in
the vast universe.
My life is quite common
as my family struggles
to stay alive in an
uncaring self-centered
world, too concerned
with themselves to worry
about others like me and
my brothers and sisters.
I am hungry, homeless,
have few clothes to
protect me from the
elements, worried
about surviving
through the scary night.

I have a lot of time
to think and wonder
why we simply do not
help each other.
My parents told me we
are now able to help
everyone in their time
of need; that we can grow
enough food to be able to
feed the hungry, build
enough houses to

shelter to the homeless.

Perhaps if we each truly
cared about each other,
treated all others with
respect and unconditional
love, like I treat them,
everyone, not just those
with privilege and money,
can live together as one.

Look in the Mirror

When we look
at our reflection,
what do we see?
Is it our physical
appearance, or do
we observe what it
is that makes each
person truly unique?
The outer shell is
but an illusion.
Our learned self-
centered beliefs,
reflected by our actions,
thoughts, and deeds,
do not mirror who
we are either.

Who are we?

We are spirit, present
within every life.
To truly know yourself
gaze beyond your
reflection and façade,
to the genuine soul within.
Only then will you
understand who
you really are.

The Story Begins

After we are born,
the story begins.
Throughout our entire
life, believing its truth,
it continues to influence
our decisions and beliefs,
resulting in many of
humanity's self-inflicted
problems and hardships.
This story is perpetrated
by the ego, our
learned beliefs.

Most live their entire
life not realizing this
fabrication is not real.
Those who never realize
this is not true, though
they may have led a
successful life, die
without ever discovering
the truth.

It is only when we
begin to question its
truth, wondering if
there is may be more
to life then what we
were told, we first

begin to truly live.

When we finally
understand little of
what we once believed
was true, that truth
may only be discovered
within, the genuine
meaning of life will
finally be understood.

Transcendence

Before we are born
we are transcendent.
We understand a spirit,
a piece of god is present
within us and every life,
there to give our lives
meaning by sharing
its inherent wisdom
and unconditional
love to help guide
our life's choices.

Though this knowledge
and love remains with
us throughout our lives,
it often becomes hidden
after our birth behind
our self-centered beliefs,
masking our true
purpose in life.

The meaning of life is to
return to the transcendent
wisdom and love existing
before we were born,
then to selflessly share
it with all others.

Sunrise Sunset

As the sun rises and
the first rays of daylight
flash over the distant
mountain top, we
awaken to the
possibilities the day offers.
We embrace the light,
visibly present to all,
many not understanding
the light also penetrates
our essence, to our
very core within.

Selflessly sharing
our light allows us to
find genuine happiness,
inner peace, unconditional
love and meaning
in our life.

Those who only see
the light above, never
freeing their spark
within, as their life
approaches its sunset,
the sun will disappear
without them ever
realizing life's true
purpose.

Reawaken

The irony of life is we
are born enlightened,
forget, then spend the
rest of our life struggling
to remember, desperately
hopeful to return to that
peaceful loving state we
once knew before we
were exposed to
the chaos of life.

Everything we learn
and believe to be true
is the cause of our
forgetfulness.

Beginning to question
the truthfulness of all we
were taught, we awaken.

Only when we follow the
loving guidance of our
spirit within though,
may we once again
remember what we
once knew. Doing so,
we will also discover
the genuine reason
for our life's journey.

The Community

All life and the
earth itself is part
of the community.
Every piece, regardless
of differences or genus,
is equally important in
the survival and continued
existence of the other.

Only by realizing this
fundamental spiritual
tenet, treating the
community with
genuine love, empathy,
and respect, may the
future for our planet
and all who inhabit
it, be assured.

Words of Wisdom

Every moment we are
not sharing our love
with another is lost time.
Every conflict, negative
emotion, destroys the
precious moments
we have to achieve
our life's purpose.

To start to understand
why we are born, we
must begin to let go of
our learned behaviors.
When we do we may
then be able to selflessly
share the unconditional
love and words of wisdom
within, as we begin to
realize our self-centered
feelings, beliefs, and
emotions are deceptive.

With this understanding,
we may then see beyond
the superficial façade
we each erect, to the
very soul, the piece
of god, within another.

Spiritual Evolution

Imagine two worlds,
similar in appearance,
though quite different
in their beliefs; humanity
is the dominant species
on both planets.
On the first world,
people are brought
up to succeed, being
concerned only for themselves.
They struggle to make
money, fight wars to
protect their wealth,
allow children to
needlessly die of
hunger, indifference.
They discover hate,
fear, prejudice.

On the second world,
their beliefs are
quite different.
Here, everyone is
taught from the
moment of their birth
the importance of every
life, understanding no
one life, regardless
of our differences or

accomplishments, is
better, more important
than another's.
They are brought up to
care equally about
everyone, including
all other forms of life
and the planet itself.
They freely share
everything, including
their inherent love,
making sure everyone
is helped in their
time of need.
They know neither
hate, fear, nor prejudice,
seeing the best in others,
rather than only their flaws.

Though these worlds
are separate, they
need not be.
Humanity may
choose at any time
which world to live in.
One choice will lead to
the continuation of the
status quo; the other to
the spiritual evolution
of our species.

Only if we choose
the latter, may we end

humanity's self-centered
destruction of our world
and may the future of
our children, and our
planet be assured.

An Empty Chair

Eating dinner, there
is an empty chair
at our table.
My parents sadness
penetrates every
bite of food we eat.
Until last week, my
sister, who was nine
years old, sat in that
chair, laughing, telling
us about her hopes and
dreams for the future.
She was a wonderful
person, full of life,
joyous, sharing her
love with everyone,
even those who
looked or believed
differently from her.

She knew how
important life was,
treating everyone with
kindness and respect.
Her death was so
unnecessary, killed in a
random act of violence
in a self-centered world
too consumed with hate,

prejudice, and fear to
even notice her passing.

If only the world was
more like my sister,
loving, helpful, caring
about everyone,
regardless of their
differences, the future
for me and other
children like us,
would be brighter
and more promising.

God's Work

There are many who
have opinions on
what god's work is.
Different religions,
scholars, philosophers,
and each of us, have
differing ideas on
what it means.
God, known by many
names, is present
within every life to
give our lives meaning
by sharing its inherent
wisdom and unconditional
love to help guide
our life's choices.

The one commonality of
every belief is to help
all others, regardless
of our differences, by
sharing the wisdom
and unconditional love
of our spirit for
the benefit of all.

To truly do god's work,
and discover the genuine
reason for our life's

journey, fully embrace
this path through life,
by selflessly sharing
your wisdom and love,
to help others realize
this is god's work as well.

Our Children's Pain

Children should know
love as they learn and
are exposed to the
reality of life; instead,
they discover pain.
They see unnecessary
challenges caused by
living in an uncaring
self-centered world.
They observe children
die from starvation,
violence, cruelty.
They see other children
struggle as they are
homeless, hungry,
experience prejudice.

Their pain is not
temporary; it does
not disappear when
it is no longer seen.
Our children's pain
may last a lifetime, as
they internalize these
travesties, affecting
their future and how
they view the world.
Every action we
take as a society

must consider how
to lessen our
children's pain.

We are the cause of
their pain, allowing
them to suffer and be
fearful throughout
their lives.

The only way to
mitigate our children's
pain is to embrace love
instead of hate, selflessly
helping every child
and all who are
struggling, regardless
of their appearance or
circumstances in life.

Where Have the Years Gone?

I am quite old now.
I have a family, house,
many material possessions
to make my life easier.
I had a good job, made
a lot of money, traveled,
enjoyed the best
life offered.
Looking back on my
life, I wonder where
have the years gone?

I did everything I
was told would make
me happy and able
to live a good life.
Yet, as I sit here today,
I wonder if my life was
worthwhile, meaningful.
Though I was successful,
I only worried about myself.

Now my days are numbered.
I am sensing something
deep within, questioning
if perhaps I should have
shared my success to help
others become successful
in their life as well.

When I die, my body
will be buried; nothing
I have will accompany me.
Though my memory
will live in my family's
hearts, no one else
will remember me.

I am now beginning
to understand if I had
only shared my love
and excess with others,
then my life would have
truly been meaningful,
as my spirit would have
continued to live within
their hearts as well.

One

Though there are
many differences
between each person,
other forms of life,
our planet itself, we
are truly one, part
of a whole, divided
only by our outward
appearances and beliefs.
To allow any part to
fail, whether it be
human, animal, plant, or
the earth itself, means
systemic loss for all.

Each has a symbiotic
relationship to the
other; harming one
causes injury to all.
It is only when
humanity truly
understands they are
not more important
than the sum of its
parts, the spiritual
evolution of our
fractured divided planet
finally may begin.

Our Silence

Though we live in
a loud chaotic world,
it is our silence that
speaks loudest.
Seeing others less
fortunate than us,
hungry, homeless,
dying from random
violence, war, praying
these things do not
happen to us or those
we love, we conceal our
thoughts ignoring reality.

We may end all man-
made struggles; distance
ourselves from our
self-centered learned
beliefs about life.
We may do this today.
By doing nothing though,
our silence is allowing
for the destruction of
our planet and all
who inhabit it.

Only when we each
pierce the silence,
loudly voicing our

objections to the
greed, prejudice,
and inequity, resulting
from living in such a
world, may the spiritual
evolution of our planet
finally begin.

We Are All Children of God

Whether we call god
Allah, Jehovah, Yahweh,
or by any other name,
it matters not.
Though our beliefs
may be different, we
are all children of god,
equal in every way.
No one religion or
person is, or ever has
been, better than another.
Those who do not accept
this are destined to
repeat life's journey.

Those who do
understand it though,
selflessly sharing their
excess, inherent wisdom,
and unconditional love,
their spirit with all
others, regardless of
our differences or
beliefs, have learned
the lesson we are
born to understand.

Window Into Our Soul

Beyond the façade
we each present to
others, a window
exists allowing us
to see the essence
of another.
Though the glass
may be tinted, making
the view difficult to
observe, if we gaze
deeply with an open
heart, the darkened
lens may lighten.

To truly know another
look beyond the pretense,
through the translucent
window, into the very
soul of another.

The Arc of the Universe

All life in the universe
is connected by a
common bond.
Regardless of the
genus, planet it may
exist on, or any other
differences we assign,
we are all inextricably
related, linked by
a shared spirit, a
piece of god present
within every life.

There is a belief
humanity is superior,
its life more important
than other forms of life.
This belief is the cause
of many of humanity's
self-inflicted challenges
and hardships.

In the arc of the universe
we are but a bit player.
It is only when we
truly understand this,
realizing we are not
and have never been
greater than any other

form of life or each
other, that the spiritual
evolution of our planet
may finally begin.

Look Within

The meaning of life
may not be found in
the self-centered world.
It may only be
discovered by selflessly
sharing the wisdom
and unconditional
loving beliefs of
the spirit within.

Then our spirit's
wisdom and love
must be shared,
without reservation
or cause, with all
others to help them
understand this as well.

Beacon of Light

Surrounded by hardships,
tragedies too numerous
to list, many struggle
to survive in a self-
centered world,
concerned only with
what is best for
themselves, rather
than caring about the
challenges of others.

We each may be a
beacon of light
in a dark world.
To do so, we must
open our heart,
embrace our unlimited
capacity of love within,
and then selflessly
share it, without
reason or benefit,
with all others.

I Appreciate You

There is a deeper
meaning to the words
'I appreciate you.'
These words signify,
not only do we hear
and understand what
another is saying,
but also we see
beyond their words,
to their soul within.
We sense their
boundless love,
their authentic-self,
as our soul interacts
with theirs on a higher-
vibrational level; a
spiritual plane where
our souls unite as one.

To truly know another,
appreciate their
journey through life.
Anything else is
superficial, isolating
us from genuinely
knowing the essence,
the extraordinary beauty
present within another.

We Are the Children

We are the children
of the world.
Look at the needless
destruction of our
planet; the pollution
of our air, land, water.
The senseless violence
due to greed, prejudice,
intolerance.
Children and others
dying from hunger,
war, indifference.

What an abysmal job
the adults have done.
They care only about
themselves, ignoring
the reality of what we,
your children, will inherit.
The adults are self-centered,
ignoring the struggles our
parents now experience and
we will have in the future.

All these challenging
things need not occur.
It is a choice to pursue
this path; a path that is
unsustainable for us.

It is time the adults
step aside, allowing
your children to
decide our future.
If we are given a
chance, we will
embrace peace
instead of war,
compassion instead
of indifference, and
love instead of hate.

The Script

Everything we learn
in life is not real; it
is a play, in which we
all have our bit roles.
Though we do have
choices as to how
we project ourselves
during our lives and
the direction our life
will take, those leading
to discovering our
authentic-self, present
within every life, are
difficult to uncover.
They are hidden deep
within each of us,
behind the learned
façade we project
to the other actors
in the play.

It is difficult to
penetrate the
pretense or alter our
lines in the play, but
it is not impossible.
We awake when we first
begin to understand this.
We become enlightened

when we change,
ad-lib, our dialogue,
now accepting and
sharing the inherent
wisdom and unconditional
loving messages of our
spirit within, instead
of only the false
learned self-centered
ones written in the script.

How Many More Must Die?

Our children are dying.
War, hunger, disease,
all preventable,
extinguish their
life before their
appointed time.
Innocent, they die from
indiscriminate violence,
lack of medicine or
food, seeing their
slight bodies lifeless
in a world too self-
centered to care or notice.
Their faces covered
in blood, ribs protruding
through their skin, they
lie quietly as they wait
to take their last breath.

How many more must die?
To stop this carnage,
regardless of our differences,
we must selflessly embrace
all our children and each
other, with compassion
instead of indifference,
acceptance instead of
prejudice, love instead of
hate, spirit instead of ego.

To Effect Change

Hunger, homelessness,
climate change; these
man-made problems
and many others may
be mitigated now.
Technology exists to end
these scourges today.
Hate, fear, prejudice;
these man-made learned
negative emotions
and many others may
be ended as well.
They exist due to living
in a self-centered world
of greed, worrying only
about our own success
and happiness, having
little concern for any others.

Genuine change may
only occur though,
when we all accept
the spiritual path of love,
compassion, and empathy,
equally respecting the
needs of every life,
regardless of our differences,
rather than only the
yearnings of our own.

Look Up

We must no longer
ignore those who
are struggling.
In different circumstances,
it could be us
instead of them.
When we walk by
someone homeless,
hungry, dressed in
tattered clothes,
refugees from war or
political discourse, many
gaze away, not wanting
to look or confront the
struggles and pain
they are experiencing.
It is simply easier to
ignore them, so the
bubble of security we
exist in does not rupture.

To bring genuine change
we must burst our
protective shell, confronting
the truth and reality.
Everyone suffering for
any reason must no
longer go unnoticed.
We must all look up,

selflessly helping
all in need.
Only then may we
begin to awaken to
life's true potential.

We Each Have Value

Though it may be
difficult to recognize,
every life has value.
One should never
be judged by their
appearance, beliefs,
or façade they present
to the world.

Within each life there
is a spirit, a piece of
god connecting each
of us to the other.
It is here our true
value resides.

Look past what you
see to know the true
worth of another.

What Are Our Dreams?

When we dream
of a brighter future,
what do we see?
Many see a time
when they do not
have to worry
about money.
Others see a world
living in peace,
where the many
challenges and
prejudices of
humanity have
been alleviated.

Though being financially
secure would make
life easier, unless
the world unites,
selflessly sharing
its unconditional love
and excess equally
with all, our wonderful
dreams may turn into
a nightmare, as there
may be little left of
our planet to spend our
newfound riches on.

I Am

I am black, white,
Hispanic, Asian,
Muslim, Buddhist,
rich, poor, or any of
the many other differences
we assign to each other.
If we judge another by
their traits or beliefs,
we remain asleep.

When we begin to
wonder if some of
these differences may
not be important, we awaken.
Though we are all
different, every life is
connected, inextricably
linked together by a
universal spirit within,
joining each of us
to the other.

Despite our achievements,
appearance, beliefs, or
genus, we have never
been better, our life
more important than
another's, each too
having a spirit, a piece
of god within them as well.

Finding Genuine Meaning and Happiness

Though money makes
life easier, allowing us
to worry less about
our basic necessities,
it does not assure we
will find inner peace,
true love, or discover
genuine meaning and
happiness in our life.

There are those who
have been impoverished,
yet have been able
to discover these
sought out emotions.
And others, who have
been wealthy, never
able to find them.

Genuine meaning and
happiness may not be
found in a self-centered world.
It must first be uncovered
within, then must be
selflessly shared to help
others find meaning and
happiness in their
lives as well.

Words Are Not Necessary

When we speak to
another, our words
are often influenced
by our beliefs and
experiences in life.
Our thoughts and
prose therefore arise
mostly from our mind,
rather than from the
inherent unbiased loving
feelings and emotions
within our heart.

A simple touch, loving
look, warm embrace,
connects us to someone
more than words
could ever express.
To genuinely know
another, letting them
know how you truly
feel, gaze deeply into
their soul, speaking
silently from your
heart, rather than
loudly from your mind.

A Good Life

Though life can be
quite challenging, how we
live it does not need to be.
It is our perceptions,
beliefs, and expectations,
about what we desire
that is the root cause of
not only many of the
difficulties life presents
us, but the numerous
hardships experienced
by many around the
world as well.

It does not take money,
material possessions,
luxury, to live a good life.
Though these things may
make our life easier,
living a good life has
little to do with any of them.
Rather, a good life may
only be experienced
when we uncover the
genuine reason for our
life's journey.
Once we truly
understand this,
life's difficulties

begin to melt away.

We have always had the
answers to living a good
life; we were only
looking for them in
the wrong place.
When we selflessly
share the inherent
wisdom and unconditional
love of our spirit, a
piece of god within,
with all others, our
life's challenges will
lessen, as we will have
understood the genuine
meaning of life.

The Philosophy of Humanity

There have been
many philosophers
throughout the ages
whose varying views
of humanity have
attempted to teach
us the meaning of life.
For most of us, their
words and opinions
are often confusing,
worded in a fashion
not easily understood
by the average person.

In truth, humanity is
on a spiritual journey,
contained in a human
shell, inside which
a spirit, a piece
of god is present.
Many of humanity's
self-inflicted problems
and challenges in life
occur when they
embrace their human
self-centered beliefs,
rather than the innate
wisdom and unconditional
loving beliefs of their

spirit within.

Only when humanity
truly understands this
and follows the guidance
of its spirit, rather than
ego, will their problems
start to mitigate and our
world begin to heal.

An Existential Time in History

The past is replete
with examples of
tragedies resulting
from the dominance
of humanity over
all other forms of
life, each other, and
our planet itself.
Though these challenges
were formidable, our
world today is at a
precipice, overlooking
a deep abyss.
The threats and problems
resulting from our
indifference are so
vast, humanity and the
earth itself, may not endure.

This existential crisis may
only be averted by
embracing the spiritual
path through life, selflessly
sharing the wisdom and
unconditional love,
present within each
of us, to help improve
life for all.

Humanity still has a
choice and the ability
to avert descending
into the abyss.
Though if we do not
choose to change the
direction we are currently
following, in a very
short time, the decision
whether to step back
from the edge may
be made for us.

We Are All One

Every life, though
seeming different,
regardless of genus,
beliefs, appearance,
or any of the hundreds
of other differences
humanity assigns to
others, is part of a
universal collective,
intimately linked by
a spirit, a piece of god
present within each.

We are all one,
united by our spirit,
whose innate wisdom
and unconditional
love is meant to be
selflessly shared to
benefit all.

A Reflection of Our Heart

She is four feet,
eleven inches tall,
weighs ninety pounds,
wears tattered clothes,
lives in a small abode
with a dirt floor, the roof
leaking when it rains.
As you can probably tell,
she is quite poor, often
eating just one small
meal a day for sustenance.

Yet despite this, she is
the biggest person
I have ever known.
She shares the little
she has with those
even less fortunate
then she is, spends
her days selflessly
helping all others
in need, regardless
of their beliefs,
appearance, or if
they are strangers.
Her love is shared,
without reason or
benefit, to make others'
lives easier, realizing

the genuine importance
and value of each.

Big has absolutely
nothing to do with size,
wealth, prestige.
In reality, it is simply
a reflection of our heart.

Living in a Bipolar World

Living in an intense
fast paced world, our
thoughts often race as
we attempt to juggle
many different situations
we each face every day.
We often rely on our past
beliefs to make hasty
choices as to what we
will say or do.

Depending on our
experiences, our
decisions may be
appropriate or they may
cause harm to another.
At times such as these,
it may be best to
remain silent, allowing
our frantic thoughts to
settle, listening intently
instead to the wisdom
and quiet loving
messages within.

Only by controlling our
manic reactions to the
world, attempting to
suppress its negative

desires and actions,
may change not only
improve our own lives,
but the lives of all others
on our planet as well.

Never Harm Another

There is never cause
to harm another.
Regardless of the reason,
provocation, or desire to
demonstrate our superiority
to others, the harm
adversely affects us
as much as those
we inflict it on.
It means little if the
slight is physical, verbal,
or in any other manner.

When we treat another
with disdain, not respecting
their equal right to exist,
we add to the severe
harmful burden we
are placing on each
other and the world.

We are alive to selflessly
share our inherent wisdom
and unconditional love, our
spirit, with all others.
Anything else, in pursuit
of our own gratification,
will only further distance us
from our genuine life's purpose.

Open Your Mind

A spirit, a piece
of god is present
within every life.
Hearing, accepting,
and selflessly sharing
its innate wisdom and
unconditional loving
messages with all others
is the reason we are
alive; the meaning of life.

The spirit's messages
though, are often silenced
due the influence of
the dominate ego, our
self-centered beliefs.
When this happens
stress and anxiety may
result from the spirit
trying to be heard and
the ego attempting to
suppress its messages.

When we open our mind
to the possibility of this
truth, we begin a journey
to discover the genuine
reason we were born.

Look Past the Ego

When we speak to
another, our words
are spoken mostly
through the lens
of the self, rather
than through
the connectivity
of the heart.
As such, there are
often ulterior motives
involved, resulting from
what we have each learned
throughout our life and
what we hope to gain
for ourselves through
our interaction.

This often results in each
trying to convince the
other to do or accept
something we both
believe is right.
Our messages to each
other, therefore, are
mostly superficial,
dictated by our needs,
beliefs, and desires ingrained
in us by society as
we are growing up.

To truly know another,
look past the ego, open
your heart, speak to each
other by embracing the
wisdom and unconditional
loving beliefs of
the spirit within.
For this is who
we truly are.

The Self

The self, our learned
beliefs, is created
after we are born.
It is there to teach
us how to survive
in the world.
Though the self is
important and will
accompany each of us
throughout our life,
it provides us with
a false narrative.
Its directive is to
convince us meaning
and success may be
found in a self-centered
world; it cannot.

Some, during their life,
may start to sense a
presence within,
beginning them to
question the self's truth.
As they slowly realize
its truth was wrong, they
begin on a journey to
discover their true
purpose in life.

Our Emotions

Pseudo emotions are
superficial learned
reactions to different
life situations.
After we are born,
by watching movies,
reading books,
experiencing life,
we learn what these
emotions are.
Pseudo emotions are
about us; they are
shared protecting
our self-interest.

Many live their entire
lives adopting these
feelings, insulating
them from ever being
able to truly know another.
Pseudo emotions will
only lead to loneliness,
isolation, and suffering.

Inherent emotions are
authentic loving emotions
present within each life.
These emotions allow
us to get close to others,

getting to truly know
someone on a much
deeper genuine level.
Inherent emotions
are about everyone.
They are shared with
genuine concern for
what is best for another.

It is only when we awaken
may we begin to share
our inherent emotions and
no longer be alone.
For it is then we will
truly know each other.

A World on Fire

The intense heat
radiates in every
direction as the
world burns, leaving
ashes in its wake.
The orange flames
leap into the sky as we
helplessly try to mitigate
its devastating effects
on the earth and all
its inhabitants.

Though fire is a
metaphor, our world
is in grave danger.
Humanity is the spark,
with innumerable problems
caused by their inaction
and lack of respect for
not only our planet,
but all life in it, and
each other as well.

Only changing our
fundamental self-centered
beliefs, by equally caring
for others, and the earth
that sustains us all, may
we extinguish the flames,

before our home
is no longer recognizable.

What is the Devil?

Perhaps the devil is
the ego, our self-centered
beliefs, gaining strength
and direction from
everything we learn
since birth, struggling
to dominate the
host it resides in.
This may result
in stress, anxiety,
and uncertainty.

Though the ego is
necessary for survival,
it is only when its
presence is relegated
to a lesser role,
secondary to the
spirit, our stress and
anxiety may be
mitigated, and true
happiness, inner
peace, and meaning
be discovered.

Our Children Deserve Better

Living in a dangerous
insensitive world, where
war, inequity, prejudice
dominate, believing
these things are an
inevitable part of life
unable to be changed,
many feel hopeless.

These challenges,
however, are created
by humanity to prove
our dominance not only
over all forms of life,
but each other as well.
Though most have
resigned themselves
to this fate, our children
deserve better.

It is up to each of us
to confront our apathy
embracing peace,
acceptance, and love,
rather than war, prejudice,
and hate.
Only then may our
children live in a world
they may truly thrive in.

True Happiness

With enlightenment there
is an awareness true
happiness may not be
found in the self-
centered world.
It must first be
discovered within,
then selflessly shared
to help others find
true happiness in
their life as well.

When we truly
understand this our
lives will change forever.
We now realize what
we once thought was
important really was not,
and the happiness we
found in the world from
everything we were taught
would bring us joy, was
simply an illusion.

Living in an Enlightened World

Imagine a world where
adults and children lived
together, shared everything,
and concern for each other
replaced the struggles of
living in a competitive world.

In such a realm, all resources
would be equally shared,
and the children would be
tutored by the collective
to selflessly embrace the
wisdom and unconditional
loving beliefs we
each possess within.
They would be raised
knowing and understanding
the value of sharing,
compassion, and love.
There would be
cooperation between
everyone; no one
would be without shelter,
hungry, or alone.
Food would be grown
collectively with everyone
equally sharing the
bounties of the earth.
Decisions would be

made by the community,
always considering what
was best for all, rather
than just the individual.

The sway and importance
of money and material
possessions mean little here.
Those who have more
would share their excess
with others.
In this world no one
would be considered
better than another.
The color of their skin,
religion, ideologies,
appearance, or any other
self-centered differences
would not matter.

This is what living in
an enlightened society
would be like.
A place where we all
truly care and help
each other, recognizing
the value of every life.

Triggers in Life

No matter how much
we try to forget the
past, certain triggers
in life often bring back
terrible memories
and emotions we felt
when we were young.

It is not until we realize
and accept those self-
centered feelings and
memories affecting our
lives were a distraction
by the ego, our learned
beliefs, to enforce its
will on us, that we may
finally be able to let go
of our past, and live a more
complete meaningful
loving life.

Meaning and Happiness

There are some people
who are poor, have little,
yet are truly happy, content.
And others, who have
succeeded in life, who
are depressed, unhappy,
struggling within.

Why?

Perhaps it is because
the former have found
meaning and happiness,
not from the material
pleasures in the world,
but from understanding
true meaning and
happiness may not
be found there.
They must first be
discovered within,
then selflessly shared,
without motive or benefit,
to help others find true
meaning and happiness
in their lives as well.

How Do I Begin My Spiritual Journey?

To begin your spiritual
journey, stop talking,
listen quietly, intently, in
between your racing thoughts.
When you do, you will
hear one of two things.
The first is the incessant
chatter of the learned
self-centered opinions
of those conversing.

The second is the
underlying wisdom and
messages of unconditional
love present within every life.
Though it may be difficult
to find the latter in many,
it is there, often hidden
behind the façade we
learn to project.

To discover the spiritual
path, ignore the former,
embrace and seek out the latter.
Doing so, you will begin
an extraordinary journey
to understand your
life's true purpose.

The Mores of Society

Instead of helping
others, we hurt them.
Instead of loving
others, we fear and
hate them.

The irony of life is
as we are socialized to
accept the self-centered
mores of society,
many adopt these
negative harmful
attitudes toward others,
then often spend the
rest of their lives
undoing the damage
and prejudice
embracing these
beliefs caused.

What is Normal?

Violence, hunger,
homelessness; hate,
prejudice, inequity.
Are these normal?
In a self-centered
world they are.
Most passively observe
the struggles others
face daily, convinced
there is little they may
do to change the
direction of the world.
Apathy and indifference
will only lead to further
hardship, struggle,
and uncertainty.

No longer must we
accept the world's
definition of normal.
Each of us has the
ability to change the
world by sharing
our innate wisdom
and unconditional
love with others.
If we do not try,
continuing to accept
the world's definition

of normal, though our
planet may survive,
humanity may no
longer grace its soil.

A New Beginning

The earth was created
billions of years ago
when gas and existing
particles in the solar system
collided with each
other to form our planet.
This genesis was followed
by evolution and the
creation of sentient life.

A new beginning is
desperately needed
now before humanity
ends all life on our
planet, leaving a
lifeless world in its wake.
Technology will not
solve this dilemma.
Only by selflessly embracing
our spiritual core beliefs,
genuinely caring for each
other, every sentient life
form, and our planet itself,
making sacrifices for the
benefit of all, rather than
only being concerned
for ourselves, may a new
genesis happen, allowing the
earth, and all life on it, to flourish.

Destiny

Though we each have
different experiences in
our life, our destiny is a
choice we may impact.
For those influenced by
their self-centered learned
beliefs, their destiny is
predetermined, as they
strive to succeed in a world
where success is defined by
money, material possessions,
and concern for only ourselves.
Though they may attain these
lofty goals, they will eventually
discover these things only
lead to a life devoid of
meaning or purpose.

Those, however, who reach
beyond the traditional
definitions of a well-lived
life, delving instead within
to embrace the wisdom
and unconditional loving
influence of their spirit,
their destiny is quite different.
Those who choose to follow
this path are destined to
understand life's true meaning,

by selflessly sharing
their spirit's inherent
wisdom and unconditional
love with others, so
they too may fulfill
their destiny as well.

Judgment

There are those who judge
others by the color of
their skin, ethnicity,
religion, wealth, and in
numerous other ways.

All judgement is learned,
as are all other harmful
emotions; we are not
born with these traits
inherent within us.

At our birth, we know
only one emotion,
unconditional love,
meant to be selflessly
shared with all others.

Embracing the former
is the cause of many of
humanity's problems
in the world.

Embracing the latter,
however, never judging
another, will begin us on
a path to discover our
true purpose of in life.

Hope For a Better Future

Inherent wisdom
and unconditional
love come from
our spirit, present
within every life.
To change the world we
must selflessly share our
spirit's wisdom and love
for the benefit of all.

Doing so, we may leave
our children a world of
hope, peace, and love,
rather than the only world
they have ever known, one
of despair, war, and hate.

Beyond Understanding

To survive in the
world, find meaning
in our lives, we need
to selflessly help each
other, realizing the
equal importance of
every life, regardless
of our differences,
accomplishments,
or genus.

The greed of the
few outweighs the
needs of the many.
The fact this is, and
always has been acceptable,
is beyond understanding.

Only when this dynamic
is reversed, may our
world evolve and the
future for life on our
planet be assured.

What is Power?

Most believe power
comes from wealth,
having a prestigious job,
being able to tell others
what to do, from the world.

Though this is what we
learn power is, in truth,
none of these things or
anything else we were
taught will bring us
power, are true.

Genuine power may
only be found by
reuniting with our
spirit within, then
sharing its wisdom
and unconditional
love selflessly
with all others.

Spiritual Unification

Enlightenment occurs with
the unification of the
conscious mind, physical
body, and spiritual soul.

The result of living in a
world where the spiritual
soul is forgotten or ignored
can readily been seen simply
by observing the world both
today and throughout history.
War, hate, prejudice,
dominate life.

It is only when the spiritual
soul is recognized, accepted,
and its path followed, the
spiritual evolution of our
planet may truly begin.

Are We Leaving the World Better?

As we approach the
end of life, many may
look at the world we
were born into and the
one we are leaving behind.
We must each ask ourselves
if we are leaving the
world better then when
we were first born.

For every generation
throughout humanity's history,
the answer to that
question must be no.
Man-made problems causing
hardships too numerous
to list, remain, worsening
with each generation,
primarily due to living
in a self-centered world of
greed, prejudice, and inequity.

The only way to break this
cycle of despair is by embracing
the spirit's messages, present
within each life, then selflessly
sharing its wisdom and
unconditional love to help
others recognize this as well.

The Great Divide

The world is endlessly divided.
Race, religion, ethnicity,
wealth, are just some of the
unending ways we separate
ourselves from each other.
We do this to convince
ourselves we are better,
more successful, important,
validating our superiority
to another.

This self-centered view of life,
accepted by most, is used to
justify many of the inexcusable
man-made problems and
harmful emotions in the world.

In reality, though we each look,
believe, and act differently, we
are the same, equal in every way.
For within every life, a spirit,
a piece of god, is present
intimately connecting
each of us to another.

We awaken when we
begin to understand this.
We become enlightened
when we fully embrace it.

The Spirit and Depression

Depression is a challenging
illness to treat.
Counseling and medications,
if necessary, may help stabilize
this illness, allowing someone
to function in society.
Is that enough though?

Many counselors, believing
they are also treating the
spiritual part of depression,
do not truly understand
what the spirit is.
Instead, they define the
spirit using terms and
ideas they learned in a
self-centered world.
The spirit, however, is ethereal.
It may not be defined
using such criteria.

Only by including the spiritual
soul, our higher self, present
within every life in the
treatment of depression as
well, will someone be able
to not only survive in the world,
but also be fully treated for this
debilitating illness as well.

The Loss of Innocence

Living in a self-centered
world innocence is quickly
lost, as children learn the
truth about what living
in such a world is like.
As they are growing up,
they are exposed to
many injustices.
People hungry, homeless;
senseless deaths from war,
random violence, drugs,
and so much more.
They also learn about greed,
prejudice, inequity.
Their innocence, once pure
with their birth, now is
tarnished by their learned
views and opinions of the world.

To change this paradigm, we
must teach our children to love
one another and understand
the importance of every life
regardless of our differences.
Only then, may our world
begin to heal and may our
children's innocence
remain untarnished.

Our Purpose in Life

Many of our struggles and
anxieties in life may be
caused by the internal
conflict between the spirit,
accompanying each life
to share its wisdom and
unconditional love to
help guide its life choices,
and the ego, our self-
centered learned beliefs.

Our purpose in life, the
reason we are born, is
to lead a life directed
by our spirit, learning
to ignore the many
false paths the ego
tries to have us
follow instead.

We are all spiritual beings
on a human journey.
Genuine meaning is
discovered by accepting
this truth, then permitting
our spirit, rather than ego,
to influence our decisions
and direction in life.

Generosity of Spirit

When we help another,
is it given with an
alternative motive or is it
offered whole-heartedly?
Did we help someone to
let others know of our
generosity or if we wish
to get something in return?

Or is our help offered with
pure intentions, seeking to
make another's life easier
by selflessly sharing our
excess and love without
reason or benefit?

Generosity of spirit allows
us to experience inner peace,
happiness and discover
the true meaning of life.
This is the lesson we
are alive to understand.

Our Health and the Ego

The ego is everything
we learn and accept is
true after we are born.
It not only is the cause
or a contributing factor
in many illnesses, but it
does so to divert our
attention from the spirit,
present within every life.

The spirit gives our lives
meaning; selflessly sharing
its inherent wisdom and
messages of unconditional
love with others is the
reason we are born.
When the spirit tries to
assert itself and be recognized,
the ego often reacts by
trying to overcome it.
One way it does this is
by causing us to be sick.
If our attention is on our
illness, often created or
made worse by the ego,
then it will not be directed
toward the spirit.

To discover the true

meaning of life, improve
our overall health, and
positively change the
future of our planet,
listen intently, hear the
messages of the spirit
within, then follow its
wisdom and loving
path through life.

Inevitability

When we surrender, we
accept the world as it is,
believing nothing can
be done to change or
improve life on our planet.
The result of our apathy
is readily observed.

Living in a self-centered
world results in needless
deaths from hunger, war,
disease; needless struggles
from greed, prejudice, inequity.
Though it may appear there
is little we can do to help
those most in need, that
view is predicated on a
false premise, one learned
as we were indoctrinated
into the world.

Continuing to live in such
a world is not inevitable.
To bring genuine change,
and improve life for all,
we must embrace the spiritual
path through life, by selflessly
sharing our spirit's inherent
wisdom and boundless love
for the benefit of all.

An Extraordinary Life

What is an extraordinary life?
Is it having been successful
in the world: being wealthy,
famous, important, able to
do the best things life offers;
or is it something else?
We are taught these things
will lead to an extraordinary
life; they will not.
Money, fame, prestige,
will not determine this.
True success may not be
found in a self-centered world.

An extraordinary life may
only be lived when we
accept the wisdom and
unconditional loving
messages of our spirit
within, then selflessly
share those messages,
without motive or
benefit, with all others,
so they too may lead
an extraordinary
life as well.

Mother Earth

We live on a planet that
is beautiful, extraordinary
in every way.
From its diversity in life,
oceans, clear skies, it
nourishes, sustains
all who inhabit it.

Yet we treat our world
with disrespect, polluting
its waters, fouling its skies,
allowing many species
to become extinct.

Humanity has a symbiotic
relationship with mother
earth; we rely on each
other to survive.
If we do not remember
this, change how we
treat our precious home,
though our planet may
survive, humanity may
no longer grace its soil.

Life

Everything alive,
regardless of our
differences or genus,
possesses a spirit, a
piece of god intimately
connecting us to each other.

To discover the genuine
meaning of life, we must
follow the spiritual path
by selflessly sharing
our spirit's wisdom
and unconditional
love to help others
recognize this as well.

The Good-Self

The good-self is part of
the ego, our learned beliefs.
It is what most people long
for throughout their lives.
It is the part that teaches
us what love, happiness,
and meaning are.
We learn how to find these
things by reading books,
watching movies, observing
others, living life.
We see and envy those who
have a good job, own a nice
home, travel, eat at fine
restaurants, drive nice cars,
and other things we were
taught would bring us happiness
and success in the world.

The good-self teaches
us how to act and feel.
Everything it tells us though,
is an illusion, created by the ego.
Love, happiness, and meaning, may
not be found in a self-entered world.
They must first be discovered
within, then may only be known
when they are selflessly
shared with others.

Needless Death

We all will die from old
age, unavoidable illness,
accidents, or in some other
manner beyond our control.
Though it is painful to lose
one close to us, we understand
their death is part of life's journey.

There are others though, dying
needlessly, due to senseless
wars, hunger, random violence.
Dying due to our inaction and
acceptance of the status quo.

Every time a needless
death occurs, the world
loses part of its soul.
Each life, though different
in appearance, beliefs,
accomplishments, is equally
important, invaluable; their
soul no longer alive to share
its wisdom and unconditional
love with the world.
Their death is a reflection of
living in an immoral world; a
world where fear is accepted
over courage, prejudice over
acceptance, and hate over love.

Unconditional Love

The love between a mother
and her baby is the
purest form of love.
Regardless of the species,
there is a bond so powerful
a mother would willingly
sacrifice her life to
protect her child.

This love is inherent,
present within every life;
it arises from the spirit.
It is first recognized
when someone awakens,
beginning their journey
toward enlightenment.
As one progresses on the
spiritual path they begin
to realize love is meant to
be shared unconditionally
with all others.

It matters not our differences
or if they are strangers.
Understanding this, sincerely
caring and helping each other
without motive or benefit,
is the lesson we are
alive to learn.

Need to Win

We live in a world where
success is synonymous
with winning.
We believe we will win
if we are smarter, more
attractive than others.
We consider ourselves
winners in life if we
become wealthy,
famous, powerful.

To succeed, we must prove
we are better than others.
This definition of success,
gleaned after we were born,
is the cause of many man-
made challenges and
inequities in the world.

In reality, nothing listed
above will allow us to
win or succeed in life.
Winning may only be
achieved when we
all succeed together.
It may never be
accomplished alone.

Our Purpose in Life

In the moment we
completely realize
little we have been
taught in our lives
about success, meaning,
and happiness, is true,
understanding truth may
only be found within,
we become enlightened.

At that instant, we understand
every life, regardless of our
differences accomplishments,
or genus, is equally important.
The color of our skin, religion,
wealth, or anything else
currently dividing and
defining us, would
no longer matter.

At that moment, the reason
we were born, to selflessly
share our spirit's inherent
wisdom and unconditional
love with all others, will
become evident, as we
discover our genuine
life's purpose.

Why Are We Alive?

We are alive, in our
brief journey through
life, to learn about
selflessly sharing our
innate wisdom and
unconditional love to
help others in need.
Instead we learn about
prejudice, greed, and
the acceptance of the
self-centered status quo.

The former path leads
to enlightenment; the
latter to struggle
and suffering.
We each choose our
path through life and
may alter our choice
at any time.

Listen quietly, intently,
to the subtle soft messages
within, rather than the
loud chaotic voice, to
choose the right path.

The Leaders We Choose

The only characteristic of
a leader should be their
sincere desire to help all
others, regardless of the
beliefs, religious or political
affiliation, or any other
divisions there may be of
those who they are guiding.

No consideration should
be given to differentiating
or favoring one group
or person over another.
Every person's well-being
must be addressed.
No one should ever go
hungry, be homeless, or
treated as second-class citizens.

We are all inhabitants of the
world, our lives, regardless
of our differences,
equally valuable.
The leaders we choose
must recognize this,
assuring the dignity
and survival of every
person they may influence.

What Defines Us?

Are we defined by our
self-centered beliefs or
by what unites us?
We often describe
ourselves by how
the world sees us.
We are male, female, gay,
straight, Christian, Buddhist,
black, white, or any number
of other ways differentiating
us from each other.
These divisions only serve
to isolate us making some
believe they are better than
others due to their differences.

Though outwardly, we may
look, believe, and act
differently, we are truly
one, intimately connected
by a universal spirit
present within every life.
Understanding, accepting,
and selflessly sharing our
spirit's inherent wisdom
and unconditional love
with all others is what
truly defines us, the
meaning of life.

The Future of Our Children

There are only two possible
futures for our children.
If the world continues
on its current path, the
future for our children
looks quite bleak.
A world of greed, inequity,
prejudice; of war, hunger,
homelessness, awaits them
as they mature into adulthood.
Nothing needs to be done
to ensure this future.
Living in a self-centered
world, where concern is
only for ourselves, we are
doing an excellent job
guaranteeing the many
approaching hardships
our children will face.

There is a second option
available though, one
that will not only assure a
brighter future for our
children, but for all life
on our planet as well.
This future depends on
the spiritual evolution
of our species, learning

to be equally concerned,
regardless of our differences,
accomplishments, or genus,
for everyone, rather than
only for ourselves.

Our children are our legacy.
The only question that must
be asked is: how can we not
make the necessary changes
for our children now, before
change is no longer possible?

The Human Legacy

As the dominant species
on our planet, what will
humanity's legacy be
when, like other life
forms now extinct, we
continue on our current
path toward Armageddon.

Will we be remembered for
kindness, empathy, helping
each other in times of need?
Or will we be remembered
for our self-destructive
tendencies, mindlessly
killing not only other life
forms, but each other as well?

Humanity still has a choice
which legacy we will
leave the universe.
If we do not make this
choice soon though, it
may be made for us.

Humanism

Considering only what
is best for ourselves,
believing human beings
are good and will do the
right thing for others,
isolates us from our
divine presence.
Embracing this philosophy
is the cause of many of
humanity's problems and
struggles throughout history.

Genuine change may only
happen when the wisdom
and unconditional loving
beliefs of the divine are
accepted as more important
than the self-centered beliefs
we currently embrace.
Doing so, humanism will
progress, resulting in
awakening our world to
the genuine possibilities
life truly offers.

The World In Which We Live

We are living in a world
dominated by fear.
It is the result of accepting
our self-centered views
about life, concerned only
for our own self-preservation.
It is a world of greed,
prejudice, inequity; of
war, hunger, homelessness.

There is an alternative
possibility, however,
that may be chosen.
It involves living in a
world of love instead.
This is a world where,
regardless of our differences
or accomplishments in life,
there is a recognition every
life, each with a spirit, a
piece of god within, is
equally important and must
be selflessly helped in
their time of need.

This view of the world
challenges what we have
been taught to believe
throughout our lives.

We are alive to understand
and accept this truth.
This is the lesson we
are here to learn; the genuine
reason for our life's journey.

A Wasted Life

Living life to the fullest,
we go to school, get a
good job, make money,
have material possessions,
a family, and other things
we were told would make
our life successful.
Doing all these things,
we believe we have
led a wonderful life.

In reality, though it may
be nice to have accomplished
so much in life if it was
done simply to benefit
ourself, we have
wasted our life.

Life is only truly
meaningful when we
selflessly help all others
become successful in
their life as well.

Prejudice

It is extraordinary some
people believe they are
better, their life more
important than another's,
due to their skin color,
ethnicity, job, wealth, or
in any other manner we
may differ from another.
This belief is the underlying
cause of prejudice, leading
to fear, war, indifference.

Humanity's spiritual evolution
will not truly begin until
we understand every life,
each with a piece of god,
a spirit within, regardless
of our differences or
accomplishments, is
equally valuable and
must be respected and
treated as we each
wish others to treat us.

Why Are We Alone?

Though in our daily life
we may be surrounded
by many others, strangers,
acquaintances, loved ones,
we often feel alone, isolated
with our own thoughts and
desire to have company.
Even those who are
extroverts or surrounded
by family, may still have
this feeling of isolation.

The underlying cause of
loneliness is being able to
only communicate with
another on a superficial
level, one where our
definition of words,
feelings, and emotions,
are learned.

Loneliness will only truly
subside when we are able
to connect with others in
a genuine heartfelt way,
expressing our innate
thoughts, emotions, and love,
present within every life,
revealing who we truly are.

Living in a Marginalized World

We live in a world
where we marginalize
not only each other, but
all other forms of life,
and the earth as well.
In our need to prove our
superiority, we disregard
everything, considering
only what is best for ourselves.
It is a world of greed, prejudice,
inequity; of war, hunger, homelessness.

Our world is on a precipice.
To prevent our descension
into an abyss, humanity
must recognize we have a
symbiotic relationship with
each other, our planet,
and all life on it.
We do not exist alone.

To change the future,
we must end our
indifference, learning
to be equally considerate
of everyone, regardless
of our differences or genus,
rather than only being
concerned about ourselves.

Finding Meaning

Most look for meaning
in their life through their
job, family, possessions
they own, amount of
money they make, and
numerous other things
they were taught would
make their lives significant.

In reality, none of these
things or anything else
we learned will do so.
We are not defined by
fame, fortune, or family.

To live a truly meaningful
life, we must embrace the
wisdom and unconditional
loving messages within,
then selflessly share them
for the benefit of all.

The Struggle

Besides the many struggles
we may face in the world,
the battles we each confront
within often define our lives.
Stress, anxiety, depression,
are but three of the
challenges we may face
during our life, as we try
to make sense of our world.

We may believe lack of
money or unresolved
problems from our
past are the cause.
Though these may contribute
to our struggles, they are not
the only source.
Looking for happiness,
inner peace, and meaning,
through being with
another person, a
job, wealth, will only
bring disillusionment.

Our emotional suffering
results from seeking these
things in a self-centered world;
they may not found there.
True happiness, inner peace,

and meaning, must first
be found within, then,
selflessly shared
to benefit others.
Only then, may these
struggles truly mitigate
and a genuine understanding
about life's journey be realized.

Apartheid

Living in a world
of apartheid, we are
separated from each
other by sex, religion,
race, ethnicity, wealth,
and in numerous other ways.
Some believe they are
superior, not only to others
who are different from
them, but to all other
forms of life as well.

In truth, though outwardly
there are many differences,
within we are all the same.
Regardless of our genus,
accomplishments, beliefs,
or appearance, we are all
spirit, intimately linked
to each other, with
a common purpose.
Only when humanity
truly understands this,
may we rid the world of
apartheid and unite it
under one banner of
tolerance instead.

Spiritual Ailments

Over half of illnesses
may be due to stress
related problems, many
only partially treated
in traditional ways.
The more we seek our
answers from the self-
centered world, the
more stressed, anxious,
depressed, unhappy, and
fearful, we may become.

Though these illnesses
and emotions are real
and may partially be
relieved in conventional
ways, the underlying
cause may arise from
within, rather than
from the world.

To fully heal any illness,
the inclusion of the
spirit in the overall
treatment must
always be considered.

The Reason

Must there be a reason
to help those in need?
Do we need recognition
from others or expect
something in return?
Those who remain
asleep may help others
for these reasons.

Those who awaken though,
aid others without motive
or benefit, expecting or
asking no reward, have
begun a quest to discover
our true purpose in life.

Children Shouldn't Know

Living in a dysfunctional
world, where greed,
prejudice, hunger, exist,
our children grow up
knowing and accepting
humanity's darkness.
They observe poverty,
inequity, war, worrying
how they will survive
in such a world.
They see this and more
as they watch movies, read
books, and in their daily
life interacting with others.

Children shouldn't know this.
They are innocent, born
to play, enjoy life,
embrace the wholeness,
love, and purity life offers.
The fact we believe it is
acceptable for our children
to be exposed to this
every day is the sign
of a decaying species.

To bring genuine change
to the world, we must
raise our children to

respect every life
regardless of our differences,
selflessly helping each in
their time of need, and
treating all others as
they themselves wish
others to treat them.

Living in a Polarized World

We live is a world where
instead of seeing our
similarities, all we see
are our differences.
Religion, ethnicity, race,
wealth, and many more
comparisons, divide
rather than unite us.
The result of living in
such a world is obvious;
simply observe humanity's
history in its brief
existence on earth.

To assure a future for our
children and all life on our
planet, there must be a
shift of consciousness;
one that encourages helping,
rather than harming each other.
Only by embracing humanity's
genuine inherent nature,
selflessly sharing our spirit's
wisdom and unconditional
love to help all in need, may
we begin to mitigate the
innumerable problems that
result from living in a
self-centered world.

Breaking the Cycle

Being awakened and
enlightened bring their
own set of challenges.
These result from having
to live in an unenlightened
world, resulting in needless
struggles and senseless
deaths, raging throughout
every corner of the world.

Prejudice, greed, inequity;
violence, hunger, homelessness,
are rampant as the
unenlightened blindly
accept society' norms
and beliefs.
Living in a self-centered
world, they view our planet
through a negative lens,
causing them to see
only the worst in life.

The only way to break this
destructive repetitive cycle
of despair is to awaken
the world to the genuine
possibilities life offers,
by fully embracing the
messages of compassion,

peace, and unconditional
love that have been
waiting our permission
to be heard.

Finding Love, Happiness, and Meaning

It is not that love, happiness,
and meaning cannot be
found in the world or by
being with others; they can.
It is the reason we are
searching for them that
will determine whether we
will truly find them or not.

If our reasons have to do
with conditional love, being
with others so *we* can be
happy, then what we
seek cannot be found.
Conditional love is learned,
with the expectation we will
receive something in return.

If, however, the reason
we are with others is
unconditional, love shared
without expectation or
benefit, then we will find
love, happiness, and
meaning in our life
in abundance.

In Times of Need

Everyone faces difficult
situations and challenges
during their life.
It matters not whether
we are successful and
wealthy, or struggling
and poor, we believe we
must suffer these alone.
Stress, anxiety, depression,
loss of hope may result,
often impacting us for years
as we struggle to endure.
Though we are taught to
believe we must deal with
our challenges without
help, we do not have to.

By embracing our spiritual
beliefs, rather than those
we learned, being equally
concerned for everyone,
rather than only for ourself,
we will realize we are meant
to selflessly help each
other in times of need.
This is the world we
are meant to live in;
this is enlightenment.

We Are Tired

There are so many terrible
things happening around
the world we simply
become exhausted.
Though these events are
regrettable, we accept they
are simply a part of life.
Unnecessary deaths from
war, hunger, random violence.
Needless struggles from
prejudice, poverty, homelessness.
Every one of these things
and most other man-made
adversities need not happen.
Technology exists today to
end many of these hardships.
It is the greed of the few
and the acceptance by the
rest preventing change
from happening.

Though we are tired, we must
not abandon those in need.
Instead, we must embrace them,
helping each, rejecting the
accepted status quo of indifference.
Only then, may humanity begin
to evolve and the future of
life on our planet be assured.

A Leap of Faith

Those who just believe in
what they see, hear, and
can prove, accept only the
visual world of fact, science,
and acquired knowledge.
Though this group may
be intelligent, successful
in life, their lives
will never be whole.

To truly understand life
in its totality, a leap of
faith is necessary.
Without also accepting
the spirit, a piece of god
present within every life
to share its wisdom and
unconditional love to
help guide our life's choices,
life will only be partially
experienced and the
genuine purpose of
our existence will never
be fully understood.

One World

Everything on our planet,
be it human, animal,
plant, or other form of
life, has a symbiotic
relationship to each other.
Though mankind is
the dominant life form
on earth, its life is not
more valuable than any
other form of life; each
are equally important.

Only when humanity truly
understands this, respecting
all life, regardless of our
differences or genus,
will our species finally
begin to evolve and the
future of our planet,
and all who inhabit
it, be assured.

The Rape of the Earth

Due to greed and living
in a self-centered world,
humanity is destroying
our land, water, air, and
causing the extinction
of many other species
as well.
Since we are intelligent,
we believe we are entitled
to rape our world, leaving
little for our children
to inherit.

To stop this brutal assault,
we must all be equally
concerned for the well-
being of our planet and
every life on it, rather
than only for what is
best for ourselves.

Harm No One

When we think, talk, or
act, only one thought
should enter our mind.
What is best for
everyone, harm no one,
and encourage love?

Everything we each do
has consequences, often
affecting others.
We have the ability
to harm or help
others with our words,
actions, and deeds.

Regardless of the slight,
there is never a reason
to harm another.

Discrimination

Discrimination is the
result of believing and
accepting the self-centered
views of the world.
Some therefore may
perceive others as inferior
to them, their life not as
important or valuable as theirs.
These beliefs only serve
to divide, rather than unite us.

In truth, every life, regardless
of our appearance, beliefs,
or accomplishments, each
having a spirit, a piece of
god within, is equally
important, deserving
to be treated with respect,
kindness, unconditional
love, and to be helped
in their time of need.

Our Rights

Every life, regardless of
our many differences,
has the right to be
treated with respect
and unconditional love.
Though we each may
pursue a different path
through life, every decision
we make must always
consider what is best for
all, never causing pain,
harm, or suffering to another.

Living in a self-centered
world, our decisions
instead are often based
on what is best for ourselves,
rather than others.

Only when humanity
embraces the equal rights
of every life, rather than
only their own, may the
spiritual evolution of our
species and planet
become a reality.

Spiritual Law

There are two types of law.
One is man-made, created
by those in power, using
their self-centered beliefs
to tell others what
they may not do.
Though some laws are
necessary to protect the
majority from those who
would cause grievous harm,
other laws reflect the will
of the few, often to benefit
themselves, at the
expense of the rest.
History is replete with
such laws, used to justify
war, prejudice, inequity.

There is another type of law
though, which must take
precedence over the
flawed man-made laws
causing harm to others.
It matters not if the injury
is physical, emotional, or
used to demean another.
This law is spiritual law.
Its only premise is defined
by not doing wrong to

another in any manner.
Spiritual law is based on
unconditional love, treating
every person with equal
respect, regardless of the
many differences there
may be between us.

All man-made laws
challenging this perspective
must be questioned.
Though doing so may be
difficult, without ending
the harm these laws bring,
the spiritual evolution of
humanity may not begin.

A State of Equilibrium

Within each life there are
two opposing forces, each
competing for dominance.
The ego, our self-centered
beliefs, and the spirit, an
ethereal entity accompanying
every life, present to give
our lives meaning by sharing
its inherent wisdom and
unconditional love to help
guide our life's choices.

Most find balance between
these forces, allowing them
to survive in the world.
When this relationship is
static, each has influence on
the direction of our lives.
In reality though, the
relationship between the ego
and spirit is dynamic, often
changing depending on
circumstances in our life.
When we are stressed,
the ego is prominent, often
resulting in anxiety, worry,
and uncertainty.

When, however, we instead

embrace the untethered
loving beliefs of the spirit,
our equilibrium shifts
toward inner peace and
unconditional love,
allowing us a glimpse of
what life may truly offer.

The Game of Life

After we are born we
each learn to play
the game of life.
As we are socialized to
accept the traditions of
society, we develop certain
beliefs, prejudices, and
views of the world,
learning to be concerned
only for our own survival,
rather than worrying
about others.

To protect ourselves and
prove our superiority we
may do or say harmful things
to prove our dominance.
We believe we win the
game when we demonstrate
our authority over others.
This game, created by the
ego, our self-centered beliefs,
is the cause of many man-
made problems and harmful
emotions experienced
throughout the world.

In truth, there are no winners
in this game; only losers.

To end the game, we must
accept the loving selfless
path of the spirit, present
within every life, realizing
we were never better
or more important
than anyone else.
Only by truly accepting
this, selflessly helping all
others in their life's journey,
will the game of life end,
and the true meaning of our
existence finally be understood.

Investment in Our Future

Our children are our future.
There can be no price tag put
on allowing them to grow up
in a world better than the
one we have created.
We have the ability now to
end hunger, homelessness,
mitigate climate change; end
war, prejudice, inequity.

To stop these man-made
destructive actions, we need
to eliminate greed, self-centered
ideologies, and change the status quo.
To invest in our children's
future, we must first understand
the truth of human existence.
Only by realizing the equal
importance of every life,
regardless of our differences,
accomplishments, or genus,
may the future for our
children be brighter.

Perhaps it is time to try a
new approach; one that embraces
love instead of hate, hope instead
of despair, and concern for all,
rather than only for ourselves.

The Line

Imagine a straight line.
On one side of the line are
our beliefs, prejudices, and
opinions, formed when we
were children as we were
taught how to survive in
a self-centered world.
On the other side of the
line is the wisdom and
unconditional loving beliefs
of the spirit, accompanying
each of us through life.

Most of us stand with one
foot on each side of the line,
balancing our needs, with
our hope to discover
meaning in our lives.
There are times though,
in our life, we may lose
our balance, falling onto
the side of the line our
acquired beliefs dominate.
The farther from the line we
fall, the more stress and anxiety
we will experience in our life.

To begin to return to the line,
we must reexamine our life

and what we consider
to be important.
We start to realize what we
once believed necessary,
money, material possessions,
being successful, has not
brought us true happiness,
meaning, or a feeling
of inner peace.
As we return closer to
the line, we further
reevaluate our lives.

Those daring enough to do
so eventually may step onto
the other side of the line,
understanding the egoistic
path through life they had
pursued was the wrong one.
With this realization, they
change the direction of
their lives forever, now
understanding selflessly
sharing and helping each other,
being equally concerned for
all, regardless of our differences,
is the genuine path we were
always meant to follow
and the true reason
for our life's journey.

We Are All Connected

Every life is inextricably
connected to each other
by a universal spirit, a piece
of god present within each.
This is true not only of
humanity, but every other
form of life as well.

To begin to end the suffering
of so many, we must embrace
our common divine connection,
realizing only together,
selflessly helping each other,
may our lives truly have meaning.

Our Avatar

Within every life lies an
avatar, a spirit, a piece of
god with extraordinary
abilities capable of doing
astonishing things.
Though many would
consider the avatar's
accomplishments miracles,
in truth those with these
abilities have been able
to merge their conscious
mind, physical body, and
spiritual soul, to unlock
the enormous abilities
we each possess.

To further our spiritual
journey, discover our
inherent abilities, and
merge our mind, body,
and spirit, the complete
acceptance of the spiritual
path is essential.
Then it must be strengthened
by selflessly sharing its
miraculous blessings,
wisdom, and unconditional
love, with all others.

A Different World

It all begins when we are
children, as we are taught
about our value in the
world, and superiority
to not only all other forms
of life, but to others who are
different from us as well.
Since we are new to this world,
we believe and accept what we
learn as we adjust to living in a
competitive, often cruel world.

Our prejudices become part
of our DNA, as does the belief
in our own self-importance.
This not only divides us from
each other, but also is the cause
of many of the inequities and
struggles throughout the world.

Imagine if we raised our
children instead, to accept the
equal importance of every life,
regardless of our differences,
to truly love rather than fear
others, and to selflessly share
our resources with all those
in need, what a different
world this could be.

The Apocalypse

The day of reckoning has started.
Though when it began may be
debatable, the future of all
life and our planet itself
are in dire jeopardy.
Senseless unending wars,
threats of nuclear annihilation,
or the devasting effects of
climate change are but three
manmade reasons this may occur.
Prejudice, greed, inequity;
loneliness, depression, anxiety,
add to our loss of hope.

It is not too late to reverse
our unrelenting advance
toward Armageddon.
We each may help bring
the needed change to alter
the course of humanity.
To do so though, we must
no longer allow the self-
centered beliefs of the
world to dominate our lives,
replacing them instead with
the loving selfless beliefs
of our spirit within.

Unconditional

Unconditional is giving
selflessly, without motive
or reward, to another.
Anything else, though
perhaps well-intentioned,
is conditional, allowing
us to receive benefit.

All learned emotions,
including love, are provisional.
Only inherent emotions,
existing within every life,
will not only allow us to
truly experience our
authentic emotions, but
also to discover genuine
meaning in our lives as well.

Immunizing Ourselves

With all the terrible things
happening in the world,
the only way we can
survive is to inoculate
ourselves from reality,
praying these things
will not happen to
us or those we love.
We therefore become
fatalistic, accepting
these hardships as an
inevitable part of life;
they are not.

War, hunger, homelessness;
greed, prejudice, inequity,
need not exist.
Only when humanity truly
realizes this and commit to
genuine change, will these
injustices mitigate and the
spiritual evolution of
our planet finally begin.

The World of a Dog

If we raise our dogs with
love, imagine a world
where everyone we saw
and everything we did
were seen through
the eyes of a dog.
There would be abundant
love, shared joyously, simply
in exchange for love returned.
No hate, prejudice, inequality;
no learned artificial barriers erected.
Ethnicity, color, sex, would
not matter; each would be
accepted without judgement.

It is ironic, though we
consider dogs to not be
as intelligent as mankind,
they are far more spiritually
evolved than us.
We all could learn
much from our pets.
Adopting their actions and
unconditional love would
help not only end many
manmade struggles around
the world, but also further our
own spiritual evolution as well.

Fate and Destiny

When we are born, though
our fate may have been
predetermined, our
destiny has not been.
How we reach our final
destination depends on
us, as we search endlessly
in the self-centered
world for meaning.
The answers we seek though,
may not be found there.

Those who believe they will,
though they may have led a
successful life, their fate and
destiny will be the same, as
they continue to do everything
they learned will make
their life worthwhile.

It is only those who challenge
the status quo, realizing their
destiny may be altered by
embracing the innate wisdom
and quiet messages of
unconditional love within who
will truly understand life's
meaning and be able to
separate their fate and

destiny by selflessly sharing
their spirit's wisdom and
love for the benefit of all.

Change

Living in a culture of
fear, hate, prejudice; of
war, hunger, inequity,
change must come
from us all.
We must not wait for
someone else to initiate
the spiritual transformation
of the world, ridding it of
the many man-made
problems and harmful
emotions resulting from it.

It is up to each of us to
bring the necessary change
to purge the earth of
its negative ideologies.
Doing so will not only
save our planet, but also
allow our children to grow
up in a culture of peace,
love, and acceptance instead.

What the World Owes Us?

Living in a self-centered
world, our focus is only on
what is best for ourself.
We therefore strive to be
successful in life, permitting
us to enjoy the many
benefits money allows.
Due to our hard work,
we believe the world owes
us happiness, extraordinary
life experiences, and the
ability to own many
material possessions.

The world does not owe
us any of these things.
The only thing the world
owes us is an opportunity
to learn about authentic love,
present within every life.
Selflessly sharing our
unconditional love for the
benefit of all, will allow us
to understand the genuine
reason we are alive.

Why is There Hate?

We are the children of the world.
When we look at all the
devastating things happening
in every corner of our planet,
we wonder: why is there hate?

We see and read about
people who dislike each
other because of their
skin color, religion, or
simply because they are different.
Are those reasons to hate someone?
Isn't every life, regardless of our
differences, equally important?

Hate is just the beginning;
it leads to prejudice,
fear, and conflict.
This cycle then repeats
itself ad infinitum, until
we are left living in an
uncaring world refusing
to help others in need.
The adults appear incapable
or unwilling to make the
necessary changes to end
this destructive cycle of hate.

Perhaps, it is time for the

children of the world to
usher in genuine change.
We may begin to do so
simply by embracing
unconditional love, shared
selflessly with all, rather than
to continue to live in a self-
centered world that only
understands perpetual hate.

Our Eyes

Look into the eyes of any
lifeform to see the sentient
being present within each.
It is not only human beings
who have consciousness,
but all other forms
of life as well.

We are not, and never have
been better, more important,
than any other form of
life or each other.
Every life, regardless of
our differences or genus,
must be similarly treated
with love, respect, and
consideration for its
life's journey.

Justice and the Law

Every law should have
one underlying premise.
Regardless of the offense,
it should be predicated on
not allowing harm to another.
Any law that permits intentional
injury to anyone is immoral
and must be challenged.

Though some laws are
necessary to protect us,
laws are created by man,
whose beliefs often are
influenced by their upbringing.
Harmful laws about
segregation, religion,
sexual orientation, are
but three of the many
unjust laws needlessly
hurting others.

We must challenge
every corrupt law.
Justice may only be served
when we stand up for
the rights of all others,
assuring the law does not
needlessly harm another.

A Single Act of Love

One single event, choice
we make, action we take,
can change the course
of not only our life,
but the world as well.
By selflessly sharing our
love with others, without
motive or benefit, we can
amplify that love exponentially,
as that person may then
share it with the next,
ad infinitum.

To help change our future
and that of our planet,
perhaps we can begin
by simply sharing a
single act of love.

The Reckoning

Though our planet has
existed for billions of
years, a reckoning may be
coming in the near future.
The earth is on a precipice,
staring down a terminal
abyss, caused by the
accepted beliefs of living
in a self-centered world.
A choice must be made soon.

To continue to live in a
world of hate, prejudice,
fear; of hunger, war, inequity.
Or to embrace a spiritual path
of unconditional love, selflessly
helping everyone, regardless
of our differences.
If we continue to accept the
status quo, humanity will
descend into the abyss,
ending any hopeful future
our children may have.

If, however, we choose to follow
the loving caring path of the
spirit, a piece of god present
within every life, it may not be
too late to step back from the

cliff overlooking the abyss,
assuring a future not only
for our children, but for
our planet and all life
on it as well.

The Survivors

After a violent tragedy,
though we may have
survived the terror of
the event, we often carry
scars from the incident
for the rest our life.
Some events are unavoidable,
such as severe dangerous storms,
earthquakes, or other things
we have no control over.
Others though, are caused by
inequity, greed, and prejudice,
resulting in war and senseless
injury or death.

Though we are alive,
these events often affect
us for the rest of our life.
Few see the pain we experience,
as we have become adept as
disguising it behind an artificial
shield, a façade, we create
to protect ourselves.
This results in living a
superficial life, rather than
one that will allow us to find
genuine love and inner peace.

Never judge another; we do

not know their journey.
Instead, we must embrace
each other, seeing past the
hollow barriers we each erect,
to help ease their pain from
the traumatic life changing
events that may have
occurred in their past.

Listen to Our Children

Before our children become
adults, while they are still
in school, they are very wise.
They realize the adult world
they are about to enter is immoral.
At this age, they understand all
wars are senseless, helping each
other is better than harming
another, and that love
is better than hate.

They also realize we now
have the capability to grow
enough food to feed the
hungry, provide shelter to
the homeless, and end the
danger from climate change
by using green alternatives.
And that everyone, regardless
of our differences, should
be selflessly helped in
their time of need.

Our children learn that all
this and more can be
accomplished now; it need
not wait a single day more.
Perhaps our world would
be better if we listened to

our spiritually advanced
children, rather than the
adults who simply
perpetuate the status quo.

Exposing Ourselves

To discover who we
genuinely are, we must
first set free our true self.
This is very difficult to do as
we may risk pain if we are rejected.
We therefore learn to protect
ourselves by erecting barriers
to distance us from others.

Some are so good at doing this,
they are unable to lower their
guard, even around those
closest to them, their family.
They therefore live a superficial
life, devoid of risk, unable to
ever discover genuine love.

It is only when we realize
the barriers we erected as
children to shield us from
injury, are the cause of our
unending pain that we may
begin to pierce its protective shell.
Though we may risk pain
doing so, it will allow us
to discover our genuine
emotions within and begin
to understand the immense
possibilities life truly offers.

Living in a Global World

Our world is endlessly divided.
Religion, ethnicity, race,
wealth, are but a few of the
numerous ways humanity
differentiate themselves
from each other.
Every difference, used to
justify the superiority of
some, further separates,
rather than unites us.

In truth, though we look,
believe, and act differently,
no one has ever been
better, their life more
important than another's.
It is only when humanity
truly accepts this, our
global world may
finally unite as one.

The Entitled

We are taught from a
young age what the
world is expected
to provide us.
We expect to be
successful, educated,
be able to own many
material possessions,
be happy in life.
We learn, to obtain these
things, we must only be
concerned for ourself,
oftentimes at the
expense of others.

This self-centered point of
view is the underlying cause
of numerous challenges and
injustices in the world.
Though it would be nice to
have these things, it must
not be at the expense of others.
A truly successful life may
only be lived when everyone
succeeds in life as well.

To change this paradigm,
ask not what the world can
do for you; rather, ask what

you can do for the world.
Those who accept this challenge
will not only help others who
are struggling, but they will
also discover our genuine
purpose in life as well.

Layers in Life

Every person is complex,
having numerous layers to
their personality and beliefs.
Affected by their socialization
to the customs and ideas of
their upbringing, as well as
to their experiences and
challenges in life, their
views and opinions of the
world often vary greatly.

Though we each are unique,
there is a commonality as well.
To truly know another, look
beyond their superficial layers,
to their essence within.
For beyond the façade,
we are all the same,
inextricably connected by
a common belief and purpose;
one that embraces unconditional
love, selflessly shared,
for the benefit of all.

World Peace

Living in a self-centered
world, the hope for enduring
peace appears remote.

Lasting peace must first
be found within; only then
may it be shared to bring
peace to the world.
Anything else is temporary,
until those with power or
privilege, end peace's
presence once more.

Only by selflessly sharing
our excess, sincerely helping
and caring for the well-being
of everyone, regardless of
our differences, may permanent
peace finally endure.

Normal

As we read about and observe
the many challenges we and
others face daily, our definition
of normal has become distorted.
Random violence, others starving,
homeless, struggling due to
prejudice, poverty, inequity,
are considered normal.

Absolutely none of this or
any other man-made
struggles are normal.
Rather, they are the result
of living in a self-centered
world, concerned only for
ourselves, rather than for others.

It need not be this way.
In a spiritual world, normal
is being equally concerned for
everyone, regardless of our
differences, selflessly sharing
our excess to help all in need.
Doing so will help mitigate
many of the struggles resulting
from humanity's indifference,
helping each survive and be
able to discover meaning and
purpose in their life as well.

Praying for Peace

Enough asking god for
help to bring peace,
equality, and an end to
prejudice, hate, inequity; to
hunger, homelessness, violence.
Though prayers may help some,
it is up to each of us to end the
plague of indifference humanity
has introduced to the world.

Our destructive self-centered
views, allowing children and
others to die from hunger,
war, random violence,
must be challenged now.
Prayers are not enough.

Only by truly accepting the
spiritual path in life,
selflessly sharing our love
with all others, may these
tragedies finally end, and
the future for our children
and the rest of the
world be assured.

We are Prisoners

By blindly accepting our
indoctrination into the world,
believing its self-centered
teachings, we become prisoners
in an uncaring, insensitive
world, concerned only for
ourselves and success in life.
We therefore strive to be
happy, have material
possessions, make a lot of
money, do everything we
were told would make
our life successful.
By the time we understand we
were never free, it may be too late.
Some never realize they wore
shackles their entire life.
Everything we were taught
and accepted as true,
contributed to our captivity.

Only by embracing our spiritual
self, present within every life,
and its unselfish loving path, may
we rip off our restraints, freeing us
from our lifelong imprisonment.
Doing so will also enable us
to discover our true purpose
in life as well.

Why Can't We All Get Along?

If we all loved each other
unconditionally, as the
spiritual path directs,
regardless of our differences
or if they are strangers,
everyone would get along.
Instead, we learn to judge
others, believing their race,
religion, ethnicity, or any
number of other differences,
make them inferior to us.

It is extraordinary anyone can
believe this myth, propagated
by the ego, our self-centered
beliefs, to boost our importance.
Not only are we not better
than anyone else, but our
lives are not more important
than any other form of life either.

Only when humanity truly
understands this, may we all
finally be able to get along.

Our World

We all live on the same planet.
Many view the world through
a selfish lens, rather than one
that has the best interest of
others and the earth in
their thoughts and actions.
Though some may feel our
contrasts are good, they are
also what is systematically
destroying our world.

There is only one earth;
it must be cared for by
those who inhabit it.
Yet there are those who
disavow our planet, not
worrying or ending the
destruction they have wrought.
We may fix this today.
All we lack is the will,
courage, and desire
to do so.

We Are Human

Since we are human and
the dominant species on
our planet, we have certain
rights bestowed on us.
We have the right to kill
other sentient forms of
life for food, despite the
fact there are now
alternative food sources.
We have the right to murder
animals for their pelts, even
though synthetic alternatives
are available.

We have the right to pollute
our planet, even though
green alternatives exist.
We have the right to worry
only about ourselves, rather
than to be concerned about
others, who may struggle or
needlessly die from hunger,
random violence, indifference.

Our humanity gives us the
right to do this and much
more, as long as we are
content and successful in life.
Those who believe this self-

serving view of life,
concerned only for themselves,
are the reason humanity has
brought our world to the
precipice of destruction.

All life, regardless of our
differences or genus, and
the earth itself, need each
other to survive; we have
a symbiotic relationship
with each other.
Apart we will all perish.
Only together, respecting
the importance and rights
of each, and that of the
planet that sustains us
all, may we endure.

We Can Do Better

We live in a world with many
problems, tragedies, hardships,
and disparate beliefs.
Though we are all different in
many ways, we can do better.

Some things cannot be prevented,
though there are many man-made
challenges that may be avoided.
These struggles result from
living in a self-centered world,
concerned only for ourselves,
rather than being equally
concerned for others as well.

Look at our planet today
and throughout history
to observe the results of
living in such a world.
Unless you are privileged,
it must be obvious
we can do better.

There is an alternative
path through life that
may bring genuine change.
It is the spiritual path; one that
embraces what is best for
everyone, rather than

just for ourselves.

Only by accepting the wisdom
and unconditional loving
beliefs of our spirit, present
within every life, may we
finally end humanity's eternal
path toward destruction,
allowing the spiritual evolution
of our planet to truly begin.

Life's True Purpose

We each choose how we
will react to living in
an indifferent world.
There are those who worry
only about their own
survival and success.
Though we must be
concerned for ourselves,
it takes an awareness that
selflessly sharing our innate
wisdom and unconditional
love with others is
equally important.

We are brought up to
believe we deserve the
best of life, if we work
hard and make a lot of money.
Those who do, though
they may experience life
differently from those not
as fortunate, by accepting
this self-centered choice,
they are destined to reach
the end of their life having
learned little about
life's true meaning.

Only those with inner

strength and courage, who
reject the status quo, by
selflessly sharing their
wisdom and unconditional
love with all others, will
genuinely understand
our life's true purpose.

We Are All Important

Every life is equally valuable.

Regardless of accomplishments,
wealth, appearance, genus, or
any other comparison, no one
life is, or ever has been, more
important than another's.

Healing the World

There are numerous
challenges in the world.
From war, homelessness,
hunger; to prejudice,
inequity, indifference.
Though we may find
temporary solutions
to these problems, they
will never end unless the
underlying cause, living in a
self-centered world, is addressed.

Only when we accept everyone
as equal and important,
regardless of our differences,
treat all with unconditional
love, selflessly aiding each
in their time of need, will
these man-made challenges
and emotions abate, ushering
in the spiritual evolution
of humanity.

It Does Not Need To Be This Way

Most blindly accept the
many unnecessary challenges
life presents us every day.
Though there are some
situations we have no control
over, such as those created
by nature, there are numerous
others, resulting from our
self-centered actions and
beliefs, we may change,
especially, how we treat others.

Rather than continue to ignore
those most in need, we may
selflessly help them instead,
so everyone's journey
through life is easier
and more meaningful.

Do Something

Many feel nothing they
do will help change
or improve the countless
struggles and adversities
so many must confront
in their life.
They therefore do nothing.
We each can change the
world; within us, we have
always had the power to do so.
We must try.

If we do not, our apathy and
indifference will leave our
children a self-destructive
world, one where their
struggles will be far
worse than our own.
We must do something
to assure this future does
not become their reality.

Are Our Children Worth It?

Though change is often
difficult, we must decide
now if we will transform
our world or if we will
allow it to continue on its
current destructive path.
The numerous problems,
too extensive to list,
imposed on each other and
our planet by humanity,
has necessitated this
review and need to act.
If we think dramatic change
is not needed, are more
worried only for ourselves,
rather than our children,
we need not concern
ourselves with this.

If, however, we truly care
about our children's future,
not wishing them to inherit
the immense struggles we
are leaving them, we must
begin to change the world now.
The only question we must
ask ourselves when considering
which path we will choose is:
are our children worth it?

Children of God

We all, regardless of our
many differences, are
children of god, intimately
connected, uniting us
in a common purpose.
When we are alive, if
we only embrace our
uniqueness, struggle and
chaos will follow.

If, however, we selflessly
help each other, realizing
our bond with all others is
our strength, understanding
and meaning will enrich
our lives instead.

We Are the Sum of Our Parts

All life and the earth itself
are unequivocally connected.
Alone we are frail.
Worrying only about ourselves,
we ignore the needs of our
planet and all life inhabiting it.
Humanity believes, since they
are the dominant species,
more intelligent, they need
not concern themselves with
anything or anyone else.

In reality, the needless loss
of even one life or life form,
the impending results of
climate change, the systematic
destruction of our planet,
will affect and change the
direction of our world forever.

Everything in the universe, of
which our world is a part, has
a symbiotic relationship
with each other.
Apart we will perish.
Only together, recognizing
the equal importance of
each may, we all thrive.

Our Path Through Life

Every life's journey has
numerous paths it may take.
The road has many twists
and turns; some more
severe than others.

Much of what we learn
since our birth distracts
us from discovering the
true path through life
we are meant to pursue.
It is easy to miss the turn to
this road; it is razor-sharp.
Often, we are so distracted
by our life's challenges
and goals, we simply
do not see it at all.

Those who do find
it, begin to wonder
if they should take
this treacherous road.
Once they do, everything
in their life changes forever.
Though few will find the
roads end, their life will
never be the same again.

Negativity

All negative emotions
are learned.
Though it is human to
have these feelings, they are
the underlying cause of many
of humanity's problems in
the world, affecting the very
fabric of society and the
future of our planet.

Only by realizing the
destructive nature of our
negativity, embracing
instead the wisdom and
unconditional loving
beliefs of our spirit within,
may we awaken to the
possibilities life truly offers.

A Choice

As an intelligent species,
humanity has a choice
it must make which
will determine the future
for all life on our planet.
We may choose to continue
on the current unsustainable
path, putting our individual
needs above the
needs of all others.
Or humanity may evolve,
embracing the importance
of selflessly helping each
other, and respecting all
life and our planet itself.

One path will lead to the
continuation of the status
quo and to the eventual
demise of existence
as we know it.

The other will lead to the
spiritual evolution of humanity.
Time to make this choice
is rapidly passing us by.
We must chose now
before the choice will
be made for us.

Gravity

Gravity is a universal force
of attraction between matter.
Expanding this scientific
definition to include the
energy required to unite
the universe, gravity may
also be considered the
underlying power necessary
to bring all creation together
as one, attracted to each other
by a common linked bond.

This force has always existed,
though is often neglected.
It is the spirit, present within
everything and all life in
the infinite universe.
By adopting this definition
of gravity, we may finally
break free of our egoistic
bonds, enslaving us in a
perpetual self-centered
fearful existence, allowing
us instead to evolve, as we
join together as one to
improve life for all.

Our Differences

We learn to differentiate
ourselves from others
at a very early age.
The color of our skin,
religious beliefs, ethnicity,
wealth, or any of the
hundreds of other ways
we realize we are
different than others.
Some believe their lives
are more important due
to these differences.

Instead of understanding
our common connection,
they therefore learn to
embrace the destructive
negative consequences
and numerous problems
this belief results in.

Only by accepting our
similarities, rather than
our differences, may
humanity awaken to
the genuine possibilities
life offers.

Heaven, Hell, and Purgatory

Religion introduced the idea
of heaven, hell, and purgatory.
Though there are many
opinions as to where they
exist, in reality, they are
present while we are alive.
One need not die to experience
them; rather it is how we live
our life that will determine
our destination.

Most of us live in purgatory,
vacillating between
heaven and hell.
We live our lives exposed to
both our self-centered views
of life, as well as the inherent
loving spiritual beliefs
present within every life.
When both of these exert
pressure on us to follow their
direction in life, we are in
purgatory, striving to survive
by seeking both success in the
world and meaning in our lives.

When our focus is primarily
directed by our learned beliefs,
though we may be successful,

we are living in hell.
Nothing we were taught
or achieve in life for only
our benefit will allow us
to find heaven.

When, however, we begin
to sense the quiet voice
of our spirit within, as
it starts to have influence
on our life, we begin to
view the first signs of heaven.
It is only when we permit
and accept our inner voice
to be the primary influence
in our life, heaven may
finally be discovered.

Diversity

Everything alive is unique.
Our diversity not only
makes life exceptional
and interesting, but
also extraordinary.
There are those who judge
others due to their differences,
not understanding it is our
contrasts that makes us all stronger.

Regardless of any distinctions
between us, every life
is equally important.
Embrace our diversity, for
it is only together, respecting
and selflessly helping each
other, that life's true purpose
will become evident.

Courage

Any action, even if not
approved by society or
the status quo, shared
with unconditional love,
harming no one, is courageous.
It is standing up, without
motive or benefit, for the
downtrodden, poor, hungry,
homeless, and the earth itself,
selflessly helping all in need.
It is doing what is right,
regardless of personal consequences.

Though many generations may
have been courageous when
they were young, they soon
adopted the conservative
acquired beliefs of the
world as they got older.
We must encourage the
younger generations to
be bold, fearless, courageous,
by always considering others.

Change will only occur when
genuine courage is truly
displayed by always putting
the needs of all before
the needs of only ourselves.

Are We Okay?

When we look at all the
problems in the world
we must ask ourselves:
are we okay?
We also must confront
our own internal demons,
often resulting from our
indoctrination into a
self-centered world.
We are not ok, either
individually or as a
planet, both teetering on
the brink of extinction.

Only by selflessly helping
each other for the benefit
of all may we exorcise
the demons that haunt us
and, in doing so, begin to
mitigate the problems that
plague the world as well.

Which Path Will We Choose?

There are two vastly
different conflicting
directions our
world may take.
One is to continue to follow
the current self-centered
path through life.
The numerous struggles
and harmful emotions
resulting from following this
path are the cause of endless
conflict, prejudice, inequity.

There is an alternative
path, though less popular
or understood than the
egoistic one most follow;
it is the spiritual path.
This path always considers
what is best for everyone,
rather than only ourselves.
When we follow this path,
we selflessly share our
spirit's inherent wisdom,
unconditional love, and
our excess with everyone,
so all will be able to
survive and live a life
of purpose and meaning.

We each choose the
Direction our life will take.
One will result in the
continuation of the status
quo; the other in the
spiritual evolution
of our planet.
If a choice is not made
soon, one may be
made for us.

Living in a Moral World

Our views on morality
often differ depending
on our upbringing,
religious beliefs, and
overall view of the world.
We each may, therefore,
perceive honesty and ethical
behavior through a different prism.

Those who see them world
through a darker lens, accepting
the learned self-centered definition
of morality, accept the world
as it is, fearful of confronting
the many injustices and
inequalities that have
defined humanity's
existence on earth.

There are others though, who
may begin to view morality
through a lighter, clearer lens,
concerned about the struggles
many have surviving in an
immoral world of hate,
fear, and inequity.

As the tint on our lens
lightens, we start to redefine

our original definition of
morality, beginning to
understand morality is the
equal, just treatment of all
others, regardless of our
differences, helping each
to survive and thrive in a
moral world where we
sincerely care for each other.

Discovering Our Power

Most people believe power
comes from being wealthy,
famous, having a prestigious
job, or any number of other
things we learned would
allow us to influence others
and effect our own destiny.

None of these things or
anything else we were
told though, will make
us truly powerful.
Though they may give us
the appearance of power,
encouraging us to believe
we are better, more important
than those not as successful
as we are, this belief is an
illusion, created by the ego,
our learned beliefs, to convince
us our life is meaningful.

Genuine power may only
be discovered within,
then it must be shared
selflessly with all others,
so they too may embrace
their power as well.

Does Our Life Have Meaning?

There may come a time
in our life we begin to
wonder if our life has meaning.
For those who have succeeded
in the world, become wealthy,
famous, have a prestigious job,
though they may believe these
things have made their lives
meaningful, they have not.

Nothing found in a self-
centered world will do so.
To live a truly meaningful life,
one must understand this
belief is an illusion, fostered
by the ego, our learned beliefs,
to challenge our choices in life.

Only when we embrace the
spiritual path within, then
selflessly share our spirit's
wisdom and unconditional
loving beliefs with all
others, may we truly
say we have lived our
life with meaning.

Are You Enlightened?

Many have heard about
enlightenment, though do
not fully understand what
it is or if they may be on
the path to finding it.
This short quiz will let
you know if you have
awoken and where on
the spectrum you are in
reaching your goal.
Let's begin.

Is every life equally important?
Should we share our wealth
and excess to help others
who are struggling?
Should we equally care
about everyone, other
forms of life, and our
planet, as we do for
ourselves and family?
Are we all equal, important,
and deserving love, respect,
and help in our time of need?
Should everyone, regardless
of their circumstances
in life, be helped?
This list could go on ad infinitum.

If you answered no to all
of the above you remain
asleep, score 0, believing
everything you were
taught is true.
If you answered yes to
these five questions, score 5,
you are well on your way
toward enlightenment.
Most of us are somewhere in between.

To know if you have awoken,
score 1-4, and how far you
have traveled on the path
toward enlightenment, simply
look at your score and reflect.

Human Arrogance

Human beings believe
since they are the dominant
species and more intelligent
than other lifeforms, they
may decide for all the
future of our planet.
Some even think they
are better, their lives
more important than others,
and, therefore, they can make
decisions for them as well.

This arrogance is the cause
of not only the destructive
path our world is and always
has been on, but also many of
the conflicts, problems, and
inequities so many suffer.

In truth, absolutely no one
is, or ever has been,
better than another.
Every person, regardless
of our differences or
accomplishments in life,
is equally important.
All decisions must always
be made considering what
is best for everyone, not just

those with wealth or privilege.
Any other choices are arrogant,
only leading to the further
deterioration of our planet
and all who inhabit it.

Never

There is never: a reason to
hate, be prejudiced, treat
anyone without respect.
A cause to say a bad word
or be unkind to someone.
A reason to ignore
another needing help.
To kill, injure, or take
advantage of another.
To not always consider
what is best for everyone,
rather than only for ourself.
To not share our excess
to help make everyone's
life easier.

Every life, regardless of our
differences or accomplishments
in life, is as important as our
own, and must be treated as
we ourselves wish
others to treat us.

Our Choice in Life: I or We

There are but two paths
we may pursue in life.
One is the path of 'I'.
We learn about 'I' as we
are being raised to accept
society's rules and self-
centered philosophy about
life, always considering
what is best for ourself,
before we think about the
effect it may have on others.

The other path we may
choose is the path of 'we'.
Those who follow this path
always consider others in all
their decisions, doing what
is best for everyone.

Those who follow the path
of 'I', regardless of their
success or accomplishments
in life, will lead a
life of mediocrity.
Those who follow the path
of 'we', however, will
discover authentic love,
inner peace, and the
genuine meaning of life.

Which path we choose is
a choice we each make;
we may change the direction
of our life anytime.
All it takes is a willingness
to listen to the quiet voice
within, embrace its wisdom
and unconditional loving
messages, then selflessly
share them with all others.

Our Responsibility

As human beings, we have an
obligation to do what is best
for every life and our planet itself.
This includes animals, plants,
other forms of life, and
each other as well.
Whenever a decision or action
is taken, this must always
be the primary consideration
before we act, say, or do anything.

Some, believing they are
better than other forms of
life and those different from
them, are the cause of
numerous hardships
many endure in their lives.

To change the world, allow
our children to prosper and
the earth to heal, we must
discard our self-centered
beliefs of entitlement,
embracing instead the
wisdom and unconditional
loving beliefs of our spirit
within, being equally
considerate of every life and
the planet that sustains us all.

A Cautionary Tale

Worsening storms, polluted
water and air, wars raging in
different parts of the world,
children and others dying
from starvation, random
violence, treatable illnesses,
unable to afford the cost
of food, shelter, or life-
saving vaccinations.
These are but a few of
many examples of a planet
and species on the
verge of extinction.

This is a cautionary tale
designed to advise us, if
we do not act soon to
change the direction of
our planet, and our treatment
of all its inhabitants, the
choice to do so may
be made for us.

A Life Well Lived

We each wish to be
successful in life.
To do so, we believe
we must get a good job,
make a lot of money,
buy things to make our
life easier, have a family,
house, or any of the many
other things we were told
would allow us to be
prosperous and lead
a good life.

Though we may strive and
accomplish all these things,
our life will have been lived
without meaning or purpose.
Only when we selflessly
share our success with others
will our life be well lived,
and will we discover the
genuine reason for our
life's journey as well.

Listen

We are alive to selflessly
help each other by sharing
our inherent wisdom and
unconditional love, our
spirit, present within
every life, with all others.
Every interaction we have
with another should always
be premised on this.

Regardless of the
circumstances, there is
never a reason to say or
do anything to cause
injury to another.
If you have nothing good
to say that reflects this belief,
be silent, say nothing, then
before you speak, listen
quietly to the loving messages
from your heart within.

Truth or Delusion

There are only two ways
to decide if something is
the truth or a delusion.
The first is to believe what
we were taught as we learn
how to survive in a
self-centered world.
Though most genuinely
believe what they learn
is the truth, it is really fiction,
a delusion, created by the
ego, our learned beliefs,
to make our lives more
challenging and difficult.

The other group, which is
slowly increasing, begins
to wonder if what they
learned and accepted is
true, may not be.
As they start to confront
the many falsehoods
leading to prejudice,
inequity, war, and all
other man-made
problems, they start to
seek their answers elsewhere.
They soon begin to veer
off the delusional path

most follow, understanding
truth may only be found within.
Everything else is simply delusion.

Talking Past Each Other

When we talk with another,
do we really hear what
they are saying?
Often, what we hear is
influenced by our past
experiences and our self-
centered beliefs about life.
Instead of the true message,
unbiased by our upbringing,
we instead embrace what we
were taught these words mean.

The best example of
this is the word love.
Love, as most understand it,
is a strong emotion reflected
by our close caring
bond with another.
If we tell someone we
love them, expecting
something in return, then
our feelings are simply an
illusion, lacking true
meaning or expression.

If, however, we tell someone
we love them, sincerely,
from our heart, without
expectation of receiving

anything in return, then
we are talking directly to
the other person rather
than past them.
This is true for almost
every emotion, both
positive and negative.

To truly hear what another
is saying, listen quietly
to the hidden messages
beyond their spoken words.

We Must Move Forward

Life is never static;
rather, it is dynamic,
continually evolving.
Though technology has
certainly changed and
improved life for many,
there is an equally important
part of life that has remained
mostly dormant; the spirit.
Religion attempted to fill this
void, though have mostly failed.
The underlying loving beliefs
they espoused have been
distorted by a human
interpretation of their meaning.
Our spiritual evolution therefore
has not been as robust as
it should have been.

To move our world forward,
we must embrace the wisdom
and unconditional loving
beliefs of our spirit within,
then selflessly share
them with all others.
Only by doing this, may the
world truly move forward,
allowing everyone to experience
life as it was always meant to be.

Choose Love, Not War

We may choose to live
our lives in endless war
or with boundless love.
Simply look at the world
today to understand what
living in a world of war
is like; senseless deaths,
crippling injuries,
innocents dying.

Every harmful human
emotion is a result of
living in this kind of world.
Greed, prejudice, fear, are
but three of the many
emotions resulting in
indifference, inequity,
and unending struggle.

We each have a choice
to reject living in such a
world, choosing to live
in a world of love instead.
In this world, everything
would be shared and everyone
accepted, regardless of any
differences between them.
Every life would be
recognized as equally

meaningful, important,
deserving to be treated
as we ourselves each
wish to be.
It is a world of hope,
peace, compassion,
and unconditional love.

One choice will lead to the
continuation of the status quo.
The other to the end of hate.
If humanity does not soon
choose love instead of war,
it is our children, all life
on our planet, and the
earth itself, that will
pay the ultimate price.

We Have a Choice

There are but two choices in life.
The first embraces everything
we were taught about
life and accepted as true.
The majority of the world
fall into this group, believing
money, material possessions,
and other things found in
the world will bring meaning,
inner peace, and true love
in their life; they will not.
Nothing found in a self-
centered world will do so.

The other group believe
following the guidance of
our spirit, present within
every life, will lead to
finding these sought after virtues.

Though choosing to pursue
the latter path is much
more challenging, it is the
only way, not only to find
inner peace and true love,
but also to discover the
genuine reason for our
life's journey as well.

Waking Up From Our Nightmare

After we are born, we begin
to fall asleep as we accept
the beliefs of the self-centered
world we are to live in.
Our sleep deepens as our
socialization is completed,
beginning to dream about
becoming successful.

To achieve success though,
we must accept the many
fears and hardships resulting
from living in such a world.
This results in our dream
turning into an unending
nightmare with visions
of continual war,
prejudice, inequity.

We may only begin to wake
from our slumber when we
question if what we
were told was true.
We may not fully awaken
from our nightmare though,
until we realize and accept,
none of it was.

Stand and Be Counted

Everyone must rise up
and do what is morally
and ethically right.
Regardless of the
circumstances or retribution
we receive if anyone harms
another in any manner, it is
wrong and must be challenged.

This not only includes taking
advantage of others, but also
not helping those who are
hungry, homeless, struggling
to survive in an often
indifferent, cruel world.

We must no longer avoid
helping all in need.
Only then, may our world
begin to evolve and the
future for our planet and
all who inhabit it be assured.

Our Learned Beliefs and Emotions

Greed, prejudice, inequity.
War, hunger, homelessness.
These are but a few of many
man-made emotions and
conditions resulting from
living in a self-centered world.
This results in accepting the
many preventable struggles
and tragedies caused by our
indifference as a normal part
of life; they are not.

Most of humanity's self-inflicted
problems result from blindly
following our learned beliefs.
It is only when we permit the
spirit to be our primary
navigator that many of
humanity's difficulties
may be mitigated, and life's
genuine purpose, to selflessly
help others in their time
of need, becomes evident.

Change

There are those who have
used their voice and prose
for positive change.
Change though, made
in a self-centered world
is fleeting, like the wind
and rain with the
passing of a storm.

Only by first changing
ourselves, then selflessly
sharing our spirit's wisdom
and unconditional love
with others, will it
truly be long lasting.

A Meaningful Life

The ego, our self-centered
beliefs, help us survive
in the world; the spirit
though, allows us to
find meaning in our
lives as well.
By ignoring the spirit,
meaning in our lives must
come from the self-centered
world around us; it may
not be found there.

To live a truly meaningful
life, we must follow the
guidance of our spirit
within, then share its
wisdom and unconditional
love with all others.

Awakening Others

Every person may
change the world.
Start by selflessly
sharing your wisdom
and unconditional love
with others, sincerely
helping and caring
for those in need.

Simply by doing this,
we may begin to transform
our world, awakening
others to the incredible
possibilities life offers.

Our Choices in Life

Every life is born with a
spirit, a piece of god within.
Our spirit's purpose is to
give our lives meaning by
sharing its inherent wisdom
and unconditional love to
help guide our life's choices.

The spirit represents the
true path through life we
are meant to follow.
If we pursue this path,
our lives will be
meaningful, full of love.

If, however, we choose to
follow the self-centered
path through life, then
struggle and hardship
will forever shape our
lives instead.

Are Human Beings Intelligent?

Intelligence is knowledge,
understanding, the
ability to reason.
Human beings have proved
adept at these traits, learning
and advancing humanity's
awareness of the world
and the universe itself.

This, however, is only
one type of intelligence.
Without also understanding
and accepting spiritual
intelligence, its value is mitigated.
The spirit's purpose is to
share its wisdom and
unconditional love to
help guide our life choices.

Though the former does
make our lives easier, it
is spiritual intelligence that
gives our lives meaning.
Without its embrace,
regardless of our
accomplishments in life,
our lives will be insignificant
and will have been lived
without purpose or meaning.

The Ultimate Price

Though technology
continually makes our
lives easier, it does little
to change humanity's
self-centered destructive
values and beliefs.
It is our focus on only
ourselves, rather than on
others, other forms of life,
and the earth itself, that
threatens to hasten our demise.

Though more people are
awakening to this realization,
beginning to understand we
must sincerely care about
every life, share our excess
for the benefit of all, treat
each other and our planet
with respect and unconditional
love, it will take a monumental
shift of consciousness
to deter Armageddon.

If we do nothing, continue
on our current path, we may
all pay the ultimate price.

Spiritual Normality

Spiritual normality is treating
everyone equally, selflessly
helping all in need regardless
of any differences there
may be between us.
It is sharing our excess
and unconditional love,
so every person may prosper
and find purpose in their life.

All man-made problems in
the world are caused by
our self-centered accepted
definition of normal.
We use this description
to justify ignoring the
many problems others
face in their lives.
Those less fortunate, poor,
hungry, homeless, suffering
from political, economic,
or social injustice, we
disregard their pain,
believing these things,
though unfortunate, are
normal in our world.

Perhaps it is time to
change the direction

and future of our planet
by embracing spiritual
normality, thereby
permitting our world,
and the future for all
life on it, to flourish.
When we do so, it will
allow everyone to find
true happiness, authentic
love, and discover the
genuine meaning of
life as well.

Put Our Differences Aside

Though we all look, act,
think differently, it is our
similarities that must define us.
If our actions harm no one,
then our differences simply
make life more interesting.
It is only when our behaviors
cause injury, our world,
and all its inhabitants,
are adversely affected.
This harm may be verbal,
physical, emotional, or
in any other manner;
it does not matter.
It is the cause of prejudice,
war, hate, and many other
destructive tendencies of mankind.

Humanity must change course
soon, before we no longer
have an option to do so.
We must put our damaging
differences aside, choosing
to embrace our similarities instead.

Though we are all different,
we are each intimately
connected by a universal
spirit, a piece of god within.

Only by embracing this
shared bond, may our
world evolve, allowing
our numerous self-centered
differences to resolve, and
our planet, and all who
inhabit it, to thrive.

Effect Change

Almost all change in the
world is temporary, fleeting,
accomplished until those
in authority decide to
modify it once more.

Only change within,
encouraged by the spirit,
a piece of god present
within every life, is everlasting.
Selflessly sharing our spirit's
wisdom and unconditional
loving messages with others
is the only way to effect
genuine change, and in its
wake, awaken the world
to the possibilities life
truly offers.

Unconscionable

Every act causing harm
in any manner, or ignoring
injury to another, is
unconscionable.
It matters not if the
harm is verbal, physical,
or if it is not trying to
help others who are
hungry or homeless.

Many of humanity's
self-inflicted problems
are secondary to accepting
harm to others as a
normal part of life.
It is only when we truly
understand it is not normal,
instead, embracing and
selflessly sharing with
all others our spirit's
loving guidance and
wisdom, present within
every life, that our species
and planet may finally
evolve, and life's genuine
purpose become evident.

The Transformation

Spirituality is the belief
there is a piece of god,
a spirit or soul, within every
life, intimately connecting each
of us to the other, and,
because of this, each life,
regardless of our differences
or accomplishments, is
equally important.

Only by transforming
ourselves by accepting the
beliefs of spirituality, may
our world begin to evolve.
Real change must first
start within, then must
be readily shared,
without motive or
benefit, to help
bring change to
the world as well.

Helping Each Other

Helping each other
selflessly is the
fundamental source
for not only surviving
in the world, but also
finding genuine inner
peace, love, and
happiness as well.

Only by sincerely caring
for each other will all
our lives become not
only easier, but it
will allow us to
find meaning in
our life as well.

Our True Path

After we are born,
what we learn will
often encourage us
to follow a false self-
centered path through life.
The spirit, present to share
its wisdom and unconditional
love to help guide our
life choices, therefore,
becomes disoriented.

The reason we are alive,
the genuine meaning of
life, is to reconnect with
our spirit within, then
selflessly share its
wisdom and love, to
help others rediscover
their spirit and purpose
in life as well.

Choosing Love Over Hate

Living in a world
that accepts violence,
predicated on hate,
prejudice, and inequity,
believing there is little
we can do to stop the
carnage and senseless
deaths of so many, we
live our lives in fear,
hoping these things will
not affect us or anyone
we love or care about.
This self-centered view
of the world is the reason
the unrelenting slaughter
and disparate inequalities continue.

It is a choice to live
our lives like this.
By embracing love
instead of hate, the
senseless demise and
endless struggles of
so many may end.
Spiritual love requires
selflessly sharing our
excess and unconditional
love with others for
the benefit of all.

Only by accepting this
path through life may
our world finally begin
to evolve allowing everyone,
regardless of our differences,
to find inner peace, true
happiness, authentic love,
and to discover the genuine
purpose of their life's journey.

Humanity's Excuses

There are many
problems in the world.
Though some things we
have no control over,
there are many others,
caused by humanity's
indifference and self-
centered view of life,
we may influence,
enhancing life for all.

Instead of improving things
though, we continually make
excuses, justifying the reasons
change may not be brought.
Most man-made problems
may be ended; it is time
to stop defending these
behaviors by rationalizing
the reasons they occur.

We must each stop
making excuses now.
If we do not, it is our
children, every life on
our planet, and the earth
itself, that will suffer
the consequences.

Our Silent Messages

Life begins at conception,
where a spirit joins a
new being in its
journey through life.
In this stage, before
birth, only unconditional
love is understood.

When we are born though,
everything changes.
With our first breath, the
ego, our self-centered beliefs,
joins the spirit, weakening
its ability to share its
inherent wisdom and
unconditional love with us.
This happens because
of the ego's dominance,
silencing the underlying
messages of our spirit within.

Most man-made problems
in the world are caused by
the ego's supremacy resulting
from this imbalance.
It is only when we permit
ourselves to hear the quiet
messages once again within,
then follow the primary

guidance of the spirit that
true change may occur,
meaning be discovered,
and our world finally be
able to spiritually evolve.

God Within

Christ consciousness exists
within every life, waiting
permission to be freed
from its egoistic bonds.

Jesus, Mohammed, Buddha,
and others were human beings
who were able to liberate
themselves from their restraints.

With this release, their spirit
became the predominant guide
in their life, allowing them to
fully embrace and selflessly
share the inherent wisdom
and unlimited loving
potential of god within.

The Cult of Humanity

With humanity's birth, its
journey through life began
with its eyes wide open.
It rapidly became a cult
though, following the
lead of those in authority,
deciding the future for all.
This imperfect system has
led to most of humanity's
struggles, inequities, and
the harmful treatment and
unending struggles of
many throughout history.

The cult is predicated on
believing and accepting
the self-centered beliefs
that determine how
we live, judge others,
and view the world.
The only way to free
ourselves from this cult
of despair is to fully
embrace our loving center,
present within every life.

When we begin to truly
understand everything we
learned since our birth has

been the cause of our
despair, the solutions
to bring meaningful
change will become evident.

What Defines Humanity?

Many believe they are
judged in life by their
success, money, family,
material possessions, or
any number of other things
we learned would make
our lives important.
In truth, though these things
may make our lives easier
and more enjoyable, none
of them truly describe
who we are or how our
lives will be assessed.

Our life will only have meaning
when we fully embrace our
spirit within, then selflessly
share its inherent wisdom
and unconditional love
to ease the life of others.

Anything else, though
thought to be important
and meaningful, is simply
an illusion, created by the
ego, our learned beliefs,
to make us believe our
life was significant.

The Virus of Intolerance

We are born knowing only love.
It is only after we are
exposed to the laws and
self-centered beliefs
of the world that we
learn about intolerance.
Bigotry and prejudice
are acquired.
Believing we are better,
more deserving than
another, is the underlying
cause of numerous struggles,
wars, and inequities,
throughout time.

In reality, every life,
each with a spirit, a
piece of god within,
is equally important.
Differences, accomplishments,
mean little.
Only when humanity finally
awakens to this realization,
may the virus of intolerance
be treated, and the spiritual
evolution of our species
truly begin.

Normality

We live in a world where
we normalize cruel,
heartless actions, causing
grievous harm to others.
We justify these injuries,
believing there is nothing
we may do to improve
the lives of those less
fortunate than us.

This self-centered view of
the world is the cause of
many of humanity's problems.
Hurting another in any
manner is not normal.
It matters not if the
harm is verbal, physical,
or by ignoring the many
challenges others face
finding food, shelter, safety.

Only when humanity truly
understands this, may our
world evolve, allowing us
to embrace our true destiny.

Author's Note:

It is my hope your understanding of awakening, enlightenment, and spirituality has been enhanced by reading book 2 of '*Our Search for Meaning*'. If it has, could you please take a few minutes to: "<u>Write a Review</u>" and recommend this book on social media and to your friends and family.

Our Search for Meaning was written to try to awaken and help others who are awakened more fully understand what enlightenment is, so their spiritual journey through life may be more fully realized.

Thank you for taking the time to read:

'*Our Search for Meaning*' – *Book 2.* Please consider reading the other two books in this series as well.

Books by Ken Luball

The four Spiritual books in *The Awakening Tetralogy*:

Today I Am Going to Die: Choices in Life

The Spirit Guide: Journey Through Life

Tranquility: A Village of Hope

The Illusion of Happiness: Choosing Love Over Fear

▪▪

A Mystical Trilogy. '*Our Search for Meaning*' - a series of three books of thoughtful easily understandable spiritual reflections about awakening, enlightenment, spirituality, & the meaning of life.

****

A Spiritual Duology: '*Spiritual Reflections*' - Two books of spiritual reflections using metaphor, imagery, and spiritual insight to explore themes of awakening, enlightenment, and the human pursuit of meaning.

▪▪

The first three stories in *The Awakening Tetralogy* are written in the first person, following the spiritual journey through life of a child, as they learn the lessons needed during their life to awaken and become enlightened. These books are written in an understandable, interesting, unique narrative, which is both thought-provoking and engaging.

To find links for each of these nine books please visit my website: kenluball.com.

About Ken

Peace, Love, & Light

■■

My name is Ken Luball ~ Spiritual ~ Seeker ~
Author ~ Guide ~

✳✳✳✳✳✳✳✳✳✳✳✳✳✳✳✳✳✳✳✳✳✳✳✳✳✳✳✳✳✳✳✳✳✳✳✳✳✳

Ever since I was a young child, I knew my purpose in life; it was for me to awaken, find enlightenment, and share my experience and knowledge with others. To reach those lofty aspirations though, I first had to navigate through quite a few unexpected detours in my life. Though I was brought up in a religious family, it did not help me hear the messages from my spirit guide, Bodhi. If anything, religion only further isolated me, teaching me to accept the ego's view of religion rather than Bodhi's. It was not until after I stopped following a formal religion, I finally was able to embrace spirituality, and with this embrace, I awoke.

Spirituality is the belief there is a piece of god, a spirit, within everything that has life, and, because of this, all life is important, equal, and connected. After I awoke, no longer having the dogma of religion handicapping my views, I was suddenly free to explore this philosophy of life more deeply. Only then did I become aware of the mask I wore and the impenetrable wall I had erected around my heart; the mask and wall allowed me to survive in the world. I would always smile, appear happy, though I would often feel intense anxiety within. This was something I never really understood until the moment I confronted my ego. Little did I know these survival mechanisms would have a profound effect on me for the majority of my life. By protecting me from emotional pain, they also isolated me from my family, everyone else in my life, and even from myself. No one could hurt me because I did not allow anyone to get close enough to do so. In turn, no one could love me or was I able to truly love another either. This superficial life, one devoid of risk or pain, left me alone in a sea of people.

It took many years before the first cracks in my wall formed and before I could loosen the mask I constantly wore. It took me almost an entire lifetime to awaken and begin my journey toward enlightenment.

After I was clearly able to hear my spirit guide, Bodhi, I realized everything I had learned from my ego throughout my life was untrue. I had looked for love and happiness in the job I had, the money I made, things I owned, and through my wife and children. With the exception of the latter, I finally realized none of those things truly mattered. This does not mean I am ungrateful to my ego, however. It taught me coping skills and allowed me to succeed, or at least what I thought success was. Though my ego still remains with me, it has taken a more secondary role in my life now, relinquishing its former primary role to my spirit guide, Bodhi.

Decisions were now required. While it was tempting to take this newly found state of being, withdraw from society and all the hate, fear, cruelty, poverty, and greed that plagues it, I knew within myself, this knowledge was to be shared with others. That is my destiny. Therefore, **I have written 𝔄 𝔐ystical 𝔗rilogy:** *'Our Search for Meaning':* a series of three books of thoughtful easily understandable spiritual reflections about life; 𝔄 𝔖piritual 𝔇uology: *'Spiritual Reflections':* **two books of spiritual reflections using metaphor, imagery, and spiritual insight to explore themes of awakening, enlightenment, and the human pursuit of meaning; and** *𝔗he 𝔄wakening 𝔗etralogy* : the first three stories in *The Awakening Tetralogy* follow the spiritual journey through life of a child, as they learn the lessons needed during their life to awaken and become enlightened. It is my hope you will read these books, and in doing so, begin a new adventure; one where you will awaken and further your journey toward enlightenment with your spirit within.

I do not know if these books will be widely read in my lifetime, though I hope one day they may help others awaken and find enlightenment as well.

"We are all on a spiritual journey of love & peace; together may we spread light throughout the world."

To read more of Ken's life-changing reflections visit his website: kenluball.com

Appendix: Our Search for Meaning ~ 2

www.ingramcontent.com/pod-product-compliance
Lightning Source LLC
Chambersburg PA
CBHW060406130626
46555CB00005B/1996